Social Anxiety Disorder

AF001520

About the Authors

Karen Rowa, PhD, CPsych, is a psychologist and Clinical Director of the Anxiety Treatment and Research Clinic at St. Joseph's Healthcare in Hamilton, Ontario, Canada. She is also a professor in the Department of Psychiatry and Behavioural Neurosciences at McMaster University. She is active in research, teaching, supervision, and clinical service in the area of anxiety and related disorders.

Martin M. Antony, PhD, FRSC, ABPP, is a psychologist and professor in the Department of Psychology at Toronto Metropolitan University. He has published 34 books and over 300 scientific articles and chapters in areas related to cognitive behavior therapy and anxiety-related disorders. He is a fellow of both the Royal Society of Canada and the Canadian Academy of Health Sciences.

Advances in Psychotherapy – Evidence-Based Practice

Senior Editor

Danny Wedding, PhD, MPH, Professor Emeritus, University of Missouri–Saint Louis, MO

Associate Editors

Jonathan S. Comer, PhD, Professor of Psychology and Psychiatry, Director of Mental Health Interventions and Technology (MINT) Program, Center for Children and Families, Florida International University, Miami, FL

Kenneth E. Freedland, PhD, Professor of Psychiatry and Psychology, Washington University School of Medicine, St. Louis, MO

J. Kim Penberthy, PhD, ABPP, Professor of Psychiatry & Neurobehavioral Sciences, University of Virginia, Charlottesville, VA

Linda C. Sobell, PhD, ABPP, Professor, Center for Psychological Studies, Nova Southeastern University, Ft. Lauderdale, FL

The basic objective of this series is to provide therapists with practical, evidence-based treatment guidance for the most common disorders seen in clinical practice – and to do so in a reader-friendly manner. Each book in the series is both a compact "how-to" reference on a particular disorder for use by professional clinicians in their daily work and an ideal educational resource for students as well as for practice-oriented continuing education.

The most important feature of the books is that they are practical and easy to use: All are structured similarly and all provide a compact and easy-to-follow guide to all aspects that are relevant in real-life practice. Tables, boxed clinical "pearls," marginal notes, and summary boxes assist orientation, while checklists provide tools for use in daily practice.

Continuing Education Credits

Psychologists and other healthcare providers may earn five continuing education credits for reading the books in the *Advances in Psychotherapy* series and taking a multiple-choice exam. This continuing education program is a partnership of Hogrefe Publishing and the National Register of Health Service Psychologists. Details are available at https://www.hogrefe.com/us/cenatreg

The National Register of Health Service Psychologists is approved by the American Psychological Association to sponsor continuing education for psychologists. The National Register maintains responsibility for this program and its content.

Advances in Psychotherapy – Evidence-Based Practice, Volume 12

Social Anxiety Disorder

2nd edition

Karen Rowa
Anxiety Treatment and Research Clinic, St. Joseph's Healthcare Hamilton, ON, Canada

Martin M. Antony
Department of Psychology, Toronto Metropolitan University, ON, Canada

Library of Congress of Congress Cataloging in Publication information for the print version of this book is available via the Library of Congress Marc Database under the Library of Congress Control Number 2025934815

Library and Archives Canada Cataloguing in Publication

Title: Social anxiety disorder / Karen Rowa, Anxiety Treatment and Research Clinic, St. Joseph's Healthcare Hamilton, ON, Canada, Martin M. Antony, Department of Psychology, Toronto Metropolitan University, ON, Canada.
Names: Antony, Martin M., author | Rowa, Karen, 1974- author
Series: Advances in psychotherapy--evidence-based practice ; v. 12.
Description: 2nd edition. | Series statement: Advances in psychotherapy--evidence-based practice ; volume 12 | Includes bibliographical references.
Identifiers: Canadiana (print) 20250174979 | Canadiana (ebook) 20250175037 | ISBN 9780889376021 (softcover) | ISBN 9781616766023 (PDF) | ISBN 9781613346020 (EPUB)
Subjects: LCSH: Social phobia. | LCSH: Social phobia—Treatment.
Classification: LCC RC552.S62 A58 2025 | DDC 616.85/225—dc23

© 2025 by Hogrefe Publishing. All rights, including for text and data mining (TDM), Artificial Intelligence (AI) training, and similar technologies, are reserved.
www.hogrefe.com

The authors and publisher have made every effort to ensure that the information contained in this text is in accord with the current state of scientific knowledge, recommendations, and practice at the time of publication. In spite of this diligence, errors cannot be completely excluded. Also, due to changing regulations and continuing research, information may become outdated at any point. The authors and publisher disclaim any responsibility for any consequences which may follow from the use of information presented in this book.

Registered trademarks are not noted specifically as such in this publication. The use of descriptive names, registered names, and trademarks does not imply, even in the absence of a specific statement, that such names are exempt from the relevant protective laws and regulations and therefore free for general use.

Cover image: © Africa Studio – Adobe Stock

PUBLISHING OFFICES

USA:	Hogrefe Publishing Corporation, 44 Merrimac St., Newburyport, MA 01950
	Phone 978 255 3700; E-mail customersupport@hogrefe.com
EUROPE:	Hogrefe Publishing GmbH, Merkelstr. 3, 37085 Göttingen, Germany
	Phone +49 551 99950 0, Fax +49 551 99950 111; E-mail publishing@hogrefe.com

SALES & DISTRIBUTION

USA:	Hogrefe Publishing, Customer Services Department,
	30 Amberwood Parkway, Ashland, OH 44805
	Phone 800 228 3749, Fax 419 281 6883; E-mail customersupport@hogrefe.com
UK:	Hogrefe Ltd, Hogrefe House, Albion Place, Oxford, OX1 1QZ
	Phone +44 186 579 7920; E-mail customersupport@hogrefe.co.uk
EUROPE:	Hogrefe Publishing, Merkelstr. 3, 37085 Göttingen, Germany
	Phone +49 551 99950 0, Fax +49 551 99950 111; E-mail publishing@hogrefe.com

OTHER OFFICES

CANADA:	Hogrefe Publishing Corporation, 82 Laird Drive, East York, Ontario, M4G 3V1
SWITZERLAND:	Hogrefe Publishing, Länggass-Strasse 76, 3012 Bern

No part of this book may be reproduced, stored in a retrieval system or transmitted, in any form or by any means, electronic, mechanical, photocopying, microfilming, recording or otherwise, without written permission from the publisher.

Printed and bound in the USA

ISBN 978-0-88937-602-1 (print) · ISBN 978-1-61676-602-3 (PDF) · ISBN 978-1-61334-602-0 (EPUB)
https://doi.org/10.1027/00602-000

Dedication

For Dr. Richard Swinson, who sparked my interest in anxiety-related disorders more than 35 years ago (Antony) and provided valuable support and mentorship throughout my career (Rowa).

Contents

Dedication v
Preface xi

1	**Description**	**1**
1.1	Terminology	1
1.2	Definition	1
1.3	Epidemiology	2
1.4	Course and Prognosis	4
1.5	Differential Diagnosis	4
1.5.1	Panic Disorder and Agoraphobia	4
1.5.2	Generalized Anxiety Disorder	5
1.5.3	Specific Phobia	6
1.5.4	Depression	6
1.5.5	Avoidant Personality Disorder	7
1.5.6	Schizoid Personality Disorder	7
1.6	Comorbidity	8
1.7	Diagnostic Procedures and Documentation	8
1.7.1	Interviewer-Administered Measures	9
1.7.2	Self-Report Severity Measures	10
1.7.3	Behavioral Approach Tests	12
1.7.4	Assessing Suitability for Treatment	12
2	**Psychological Approaches to Understanding SAD**	**14**
2.1	Clark and Wells's Cognitive Models (1995, 2001)	14
2.2	Rapee and Heimberg's Cognitive Behavioral Models (1997, 2010, 2014)	17
2.3	Hofmann and Aderka's Integrated Cognitive Behavioral Models (2007, 2021)	19
2.4	Moscovitch's Model (2009)	20
2.5	Negative Learning Experiences and Social Anxiety	21
2.6	Temperamental Bases of SAD	21
2.7	Implications for Treatment	22
3	**Diagnosis and Treatment Indications**	**23**
3.1	Key Features to Be Assessed	23
3.1.1	Situational Triggers	23
3.1.2	Physical Features	24
3.1.3	Cognitive Features	24
3.1.4	Imagery	25
3.1.5	Avoidance Strategies	25
3.1.6	Safety Behaviors	25
3.1.7	Anxiety Sensitivity	26

3.1.8	Social Skills	26
3.1.9	Environmental Factors	26
3.1.10	Cultural Factors	27
3.1.11	Comorbidity	27
3.1.12	Functional Impairment	27
3.2	Overview of Effective Treatment Strategies	28
3.3	Factors That Influence Treatment Decisions	31
3.3.1	Age and Gender	31
3.3.2	Education	31
3.3.3	Neurodevelopmental Considerations	31
3.3.4	Family and Relationship Factors	31
3.3.5	Virtual Therapy	31
3.3.6	Client Preferences and Expectations	32
3.3.7	Treatment History	32
3.3.8	Ability to Articulate Cognitions	32
3.3.9	Anxiety Sensitivity and Fear of Sensations	33
3.3.10	Severity of Avoidance and Safety Behaviors	33
3.3.11	Social Skills	33
3.3.12	Comorbidity	33
3.3.13	Group Versus Individual Treatment	34
4	**Treatment**	**35**
4.1	Methods of CBT	35
4.1.1	Self-Monitoring	35
4.1.2	Psychoeducation	38
4.1.3	Cognitive Strategies	40
4.1.4	Exposure-Based Strategies	48
4.1.5	Social-Skills Training	54
4.2	Mechanisms of Action	54
4.2.1	Cognitive Models	56
4.2.2	Behavioral Models	56
4.2.3	Emotional Processing Models	58
4.3	Efficacy	58
4.3.1	Efficacy of CBT	58
4.3.2	Predictors of Outcome	60
4.3.3	Patterns of Change	60
4.3.4	Preventing Relapse and Return of Symptoms	61
4.4	Combination Treatments	61
4.4.1	Medication Treatments	62
4.4.2	Comparing and Combining Medications and CBT	63
4.5	Overcoming Barriers to Treatment	63
4.5.1	Treatment Ambivalence	63
4.5.2	Homework Noncompliance	65
4.5.3	Adapting Treatment for Comorbidity	66

4.6	Adapting Treatment for Different Age Groups	66
4.6.1	Children and Adolescents	66
4.6.2	Older Adults	67
4.7	Adapting Treatment Across Diverse Groups	68

5 Case Vignette 71

6 Further Reading 77

7 References 79

8 Appendix: Tools and Resources 92

Preface

Social anxiety disorder (SAD) is one of the most common and prevalent psychological disorders that, left untreated, can lead to significant impairment in a person's life and significant societal costs. Fortunately, there are effective treatments for SAD, including pharmacological and psychological interventions. This book describes the components of an empirically supported psychological therapy for SAD, namely cognitive behavioral therapy (CBT). While there are a number of influential CBT models of SAD that each suggest nuanced differences in how to treat this disorder, there is more overlap among models than divergence. This book attempts to capture and describe the core techniques that are common to these influential models. They include behavioral and cognitive techniques, and examples of these strategies are described in detail in this book. This book is intended for a variety of mental health professionals who see individuals with SAD in their practices, including psychologists, psychiatrists, social workers, family physicians, other mental health clinicians, and trainees in all of these professions.

This book is divided into six chapters. The first two chapters are designed to provide a theoretical and descriptive overview of SAD. Chapter 1 reviews topics such as prevalence, comorbidity, and differential diagnosis. We outline some of the most common differential diagnoses one should consider when assessing and diagnosing SAD. In Chapter 2, we review the leading theoretical models and research on the development and maintenance of SAD, including both cognitive behavioral models as well as genetic and developmental approaches. Chapter 3 provides an overview of the key domains of assessment one should consider when seeing someone with SAD. It is not enough to simply establish a diagnosis of SAD; to effectively plan treatment interventions one needs to assess a number of important domains of symptoms, avoidance, and so forth. In Chapter 4, CBT techniques for SAD are described. Practical strategies are outlined for clinicians, and the empirical support for these strategies is reviewed. Although clinical illustrations are interspersed throughout this book, Chapter 5 is dedicated to a clinical vignette where a client's journey is described from the initial assessment through the end of treatment. Finally, Chapter 6 includes suggestions for further reading for the interested individual, and useful forms are included in the Appendices.

Empirical support for the outcome of CBT for SAD is encouraging. However, not all clinicians have access to training and supervision in this type of treatment. We hope that books such as this can help to bridge the divide between empirically supported treatments and day-to-day practice. Ideally, a book such as this would be used as one of several tools in learning the application of cognitive behavioral techniques to anxiety-related problems such as social anxiety, in conjunction with other readings, continuing education workshops and courses, case discussion and consultation with colleagues, and opportunities for supervision.

Our understanding of the nature and treatment of SAD has been influenced by the work of numerous experts, including Aaron T. Beck, Deborah Beidel, David M. Clark, Edna Foa, Richard Heimberg, Stefan Hofmann, Peter McEvoy, David Moscovitch, Ron Rapee, Samuel Turner, Adrian Wells, and many others. Our clinical examples and experiences have been mainly gathered through working with clients at the Anxiety Treatment and Research Clinic at St. Joseph's Healthcare in Hamilton, Ontario. It has been immensely rewarding to watch so many individuals reclaim their lives and learn to manage their symptoms of anxiety through the implementation of CBT techniques. We are also grateful to the staff at the Anxiety Treatment and Research Clinic for supporting and participating in all the clinical and research endeavors that have helped us advance our clinical and theoretical knowledge of SAD.

We would like to thank Dr. Danny Wedding, as well as Robert Dimbleby, of Hogrefe for inviting us to update our original 2008 version of this book. Much progress and research has occurred in our understanding and treatment of SAD in the past 17 years, which we hope to distill and share in this volume. We would like to thank our families for their continued encouragement and support.

Karen Rowa, PhD
Hamilton, ON, Canada
Martin M. Antony, PhD
Toronto, ON, Canada

1

Description

1.1 Terminology

SAD is characterized by fear or apprehension of social or performance situations. The core feature of SAD appears to be fear of negative evaluation, though some research suggests that individuals with SAD may be fearful of positive evaluation as well (Weeks et al., 2008; cf. Wilson et al., 2023). Although many people are nervous or shy in social or performance situations (e.g., some studies suggest that over 20% of individuals consider themselves to be "very shy"; Henderson & Zimbardo, 2010), SAD is diagnosed when this anxiety becomes so intense and pervasive that it causes significant distress for a person or it impairs the person's ability to function. People with SAD fear numerous situations and settings. The number of situations feared by people with SAD varies from person to person. Some people report concerns about a few situations, or even just one situation (e.g., public speaking), whereas others indicate fear across a broad range of social and performance situations.

> People with SAD fear and avoid situations due to anxiety of being embarrassed or judged by others

1.2 Definition

The most commonly used criteria for diagnosing SAD are those from the text revision of the American Psychiatric Association's (APA, 2022) *Diagnostic and Statistical Manual of Mental Disorders* (5th ed., text rev.; *DSM-5-TR*). The DSM-5-TR views SAD categorically, meaning that criteria for the disorder are either met or not met. Of course, even though diagnostic systems like the DSM are categorical, social anxiety exists on a continuum from mild shyness to severe symptoms.

The DSM-5-TR defines SAD as a marked and persistent fear of one or more social situations that often leads to avoidance of the feared situations. The individual fears acting in a way or showing anxiety symptoms that would be embarrassing, lead to rejection, or offend others. This fear is persistent, and the person must recognize that the fear is excessive. Some individuals may experience panic attacks cued by social situations (e.g., either when they are in the situation, when they anticipate an upcoming stressful situation, or after a difficult situation). Symptoms of social anxiety must lead to significant distress for the individual, or impairment in the person's life.

> In severe cases, people with SAD may be unable to work and may have a limited social network

Impairment in SAD can be severe and individuals with SAD report impairment across multiple domains (Aderka et al., 2012). Functional impairment can lead to serious consequences. For example, one of our clients with SAD was not collecting disability payments he was entitled to because of fears of being criticized by others if he applied, as well as strong anxiety about making phone calls to "strangers" to request an application. Due to this inability to manage his anxiety and apply for disability, he found himself falling into significant debt.

Before the fifth edition of the APA's (2013) *Diagnostic and Statistical Manual of Mental Disorders* (5th ed.; *DSM-5*), the DSM provided a descriptor of "generalized" SAD, a subtype of SAD in which an individual reports fear in *most* social or performance situations. In the DSM-5, the "generalized" subtype was removed and the specifier "performance only" was added. This specifier refers to fear that is restricted to speaking or performing in public.

1.3 Epidemiology

SAD is a common psychological disorder, with a 12-month prevalence rate ranging between 2.4 and 6.8% and a lifetime prevalence rate between 4 and 12.1% (Kessler et al., 2005; Stein et al., 2018) with higher rates occurring in high-income countries and North and South America . Recent data suggest that levels of social anxiety increased as a result of the COVID-19 pandemic and those with an existing SAD diagnosis experienced a deterioration of their mental health (Kindred & Bates, 2023). SAD tends to begin in adolescence (i.e., mid to late teens), but can also occur earlier in childhood or later in adulthood. A meta-analysis of epidemiological studies suggests a median age of onset of 13 years (Solmi et al., 2022). SAD is routinely diagnosed in specialty anxiety clinics for children, validating the fact that this disorder commonly begins in childhood or adolescence. Cases of SAD beginning in later adulthood are less common (20% in one study; Koyuncu et al., 2015), but do exist and tend to be associated with higher rates of comorbidity and poorer quality of life (Peyre et al., 2022).

Epidemiological studies have tended to dichotomize gender into women and men; thus, we have used this language when describing these studies. Research using a broader perspective on gender diversity is needed. Epidemiological studies from the United States and Canada suggest that SAD is more common (Asher & Aderka, 2018; MacKenzie & Fowler, 2013) and severe (Asher et al., 2019) in women than in men. Studies from other countries are equivocal with respect to gender differences in prevalence (e.g., Jefferies & Ungar, 2020). There are some gender differences in the presentation of SAD. For example, men and women have different patterns of comorbidity, with women more likely than men to have other anxiety disorders (Asher & Aderka, 2018) and major depression (MacKenzie & Fowler, 2013) as comorbidities, whereas men were more likely than women to have comorbid substance use disorders (Xu et al., 2012) and conduct disorder (Asher &

> SAD is slightly more prevalent in women than men in the United States and Canada

Aderka, 2018). Men are more likely than women to seek treatment, but also more likely to drop out of treatment (Asher et al., 2019).

SAD is a broad cultural phenomenon, appearing in diverse cultures. Although the general presentation of SAD is fairly consistent across cultures, there are some interesting differences, highlighting cultural influences on the presentation of SAD (see Meidlinger and Hope (2014) for a detailed review). For example, rates of elevated social anxiety symptoms in the Arabian Gulf country Oman were high compared to reports from other populations, especially Western and European countries (Ambusaidi et al., 2022), suggesting that cultural norms may be related to the experience or expression of these symptoms. Rates of social anxiety on self-report measures are typically higher in collectivist cultures (especially East Asian cultures), while rates of diagnosed SAD are lower in East Asian cultures (Hofmann et al., 2010). Further, the types of situations that produce anxiety differ across cultures. One study compared people with SAD from Sweden, Australia, and the United States (Heimberg et al., 1997). Results suggested that Swedish individuals were more fearful of situations involving public observation (e.g., writing in public, eating or drinking in public, and public speaking). Individuals from Australia were more fearful of dating and starting conversations. Another study comparing individuals with SAD from the United States, Canada, Puerto Rico, and Korea found that fears of speaking to strangers were more pronounced in the Korean sample than in the other groups (Weissman et al., 1996). Research on severity of social anxiety symptoms across cultures suggests that European Americans report lower levels of social anxiety than East Asians (Hambrick et al., 2010), while they typically report higher levels of social anxiety than African Americans (Beard et al., 2011). Individuals from collectivist Latin American countries score lower on measures of SAD than those from individualistic cultures (Schreier et al., 2010).

> Symptoms of SAD on self-report instruments tend to be higher in Eastern versus Western countries

In Japan and Korea, individuals may suffer from *taijin kyofusho* syndrome (TKS), which has been described as having a neurotic subtype and an offensive subtype. The neurotic subtype is most similar to the presentation of SAD in Western cultures (Choy et al., 2008) whereas the offensive subtype focuses on concerns that one may offend or embarrass *others* rather than themselves. For example, an individual with TKS may worry that they will offend others by emitting an unpleasant odor, by staring at others, or by making an improper facial expression. Although TKS is thought to be a culture-specific variation of SAD, research suggests that Western individuals with SAD have elevated scores on measures of TKS as compared to controls, suggesting that TKS may be relevant in Western cultures as well (Kim et al., 2008).

Severity and prevalence of SAD is also elevated in lesbian, gay, and bisexual individuals (Bostwick et al., 2014; Safren & Pantalone, 2006) as compared to heterosexual individuals, especially for gay men. What is not clear is the extent to which the heightened level of social fears represents realistic concerns about negative evaluations by others, necessitating careful and sensitive assessment of social fears in these populations.

1.4 Course and Prognosis

Left untreated, SAD appears to have a persistent course (Beesdo-Baum et al., 2012), and it often precedes the development of other psychological disorders, such as depression and substance use (Stein et al., 2001). Unfortunately, there are consequences of the unremitting course of SAD, including greater lifetime disability and a higher risk of suicide attempts for individuals with SAD (20% risk of suicide attempts) compared to those without SAD (8%; Keller, 2003).

Fortunately, there are a number of successful interventions that can affect the course and outcome of SAD. CBT has been identified as an empirically supported psychological treatment for SAD. Studies suggest that individuals who receive CBT experience significant improvements both in symptoms as well as in the level of functional impairment caused by SAD. There are a number of pharmacological agents that have demonstrated success in treating SAD, and therapeutic intervention can dramatically alter an otherwise pessimistic course for SAD.

1.5 Differential Diagnosis

> Anxiety in social situations is a feature of many different psychological disorders in addition to SAD

There are a number of disorders with overlapping or similar features to SAD, making diagnosing this disorder difficult at times. Section 1.5 aims to highlight both the similarities and differences between SAD and these other disorders.

1.5.1 Panic Disorder and Agoraphobia

> Panic attacks cued by social situations are common among individuals with SAD

Both panic disorder and agoraphobia (PDA) and SAD are characterized by avoidance, and the situations avoided are often similar across these disorders (e.g., crowds, parties, or public places). To distinguish between these disorders, it is important to examine the underlying reasons for avoidance. In prototypic cases, people with PDA avoid situations for fear of having a panic attack or panic-like symptoms, whereas people with SAD often avoid situations for fear of being humiliated or criticized for reasons unrelated to panic (e.g., being seen as incompetent). Differential diagnosis is complicated, however, because some people with panic disorder are concerned about embarrassing themselves if they have a panic attack in front of others, and some people with SAD are fearful of experiencing panic attacks or panic-like symptoms. To disentangle panic-related concerns from SAD, it is helpful to consider the following information: (1) Does the person experience panic attacks and panic-like symptoms outside of social situations (e.g., when alone), or out of the blue? Uncued panic attacks and panic attacks cued by nonsocial situations are common in PDA, but, in SAD, panic attacks and panic-like symptoms are triggered only by being in or thinking about being in social situations. (2) Does the individual have panic-related concerns that are unrelated to being embarrassed or humiliated (e.g., a fear of dying or going crazy)? This is often the case in PDA, but not in SAD. (3) Does the person have social anxiety concerns that are unrelated to a fear of having panic attacks (e.g., fear of saying something stupid or looking unattractive to others)? This is often the case in SAD, but not in PDA. Of course, individuals who have uncued panic attacks outside of social situations, as well as extreme fears of criticism and embarrassment that are unrelated to panic may receive diagnoses of both PDA and SAD.

Another similarity between PDA and SAD involves elevated anxiety sensitivity, which refers to anxiety over experiencing sensations of physical arousal, such as a racing heart, dizziness, and breathlessness. Although anxiety sensitivity is seen as a hallmark concern in PDA, studies suggest that these concerns are often elevated in SAD (Wheaton et al., 2012). A commonly used questionnaire for assessing anxiety sensitivity is the Anxiety Sensitivity Index (3rd ed.; Taylor et al., 2007). In our experience, people with SAD are most likely to fear sensations that might be noticed by others (e.g., blushing, sweating, shaking), and they are most fearful of experiencing physical arousal sensations when they are around other people. In contrast, people with PDA are more likely to fear a range of sensations, even when alone (and for some people, *especially* when alone).

1.5.2 Generalized Anxiety Disorder

SAD and generalized anxiety disorder (GAD) may both share heightened or excessive worry about social situations, performance situations, and relationships. For example, people with GAD often worry about friendships, whether their relationships will work out, and how they appear to others. As in SAD, people with GAD may experience panic attacks when worrying about anxiety-provoking situations. The main difference between the disorders is that concern about social or performance situations is the main focus in SAD, whereas social or performance concerns are only one of many worries that people with GAD may exhibit. Indeed, the diagnostic criteria for GAD stipulate that individuals worry excessively about a number of life domains, which may include work, school, finances, minor matters, appearance, the future, and world affairs. When making this differential diagnosis, ask these questions: (1) Does the person report excessive worry about a number of life domains that are unrelated to social or performance concerns (necessary for a diagnosis of GAD)? (2) If social concerns are one of several excessive worries, are they a large enough problem to stand on their own, regardless of whether criteria for GAD are met? If the answer to these questions is "yes," it is possible that the person may have enough symptoms to meet criteria for both disorders. On the other hand, if social concerns are milder, are not accompanied by significant phobic avoidance, and are part of a larger picture of chronic and excessive worry, a diagnosis of GAD may be the most parsimonious diagnosis.

Another distinction between these two disorders is that a diagnosis of GAD requires the presence of several physical symptoms including trouble sleeping, muscle tension, and feelings of restlessness. These symptoms are often present in any anxious client but are not necessary for a diagnosis of SAD.

1.5.3 Specific Phobia

SAD may be confused with certain specific phobias, including fears of crowded or closed-in places (claustrophobia), like a crowded elevator or movie theater, since both of these phobia types may include avoidance of certain public places. To distinguish between SAD and claustrophobia, it is important to ask about the underlying beliefs that are associated with the person's fear. In claustrophobia, the focus of the fear is on the possibility of being unable to breathe or to escape from the situation. In SAD, the focus of the fear is typically on being observed by others, being embarrassed, or humiliated. As with PDA, someone with claustrophobia may report that part of their fear is the embarrassment about leaving or passing out in front of others. Again, it is important to look at the spectrum of symptoms reported (a broader range of social concerns would be expected in SAD), as well as the proportion of fear attributed to embarrassment versus a physical catastrophe (which would likely be a stronger fear in claustrophobia).

1.5.4 Depression

There are two forms of depression that share some overlapping features with SAD. Major depressive disorder is characterized by depressed mood or loss of interest in activities for at least 2 weeks, accompanied by other symptoms of depression including appetite changes, sleep changes, feelings of worthlessness, low energy, difficulty concentrating, and suicidal ideation or attempts. Persistent depressive disorder has many similar symptoms as major depressive disorder, but the symptoms are more chronic (lasting a minimum of 2 years). Both forms of depression and SAD may involve withdrawal and avoidance of situations such as going out with friends, socializing, or attending work or school. However, this avoidance is fear based in SAD and is more often fueled by low energy and low motivation in depression. In addition, people who experience social withdrawal related to depression typically report feeling comfortable in social situations when they are not feeling depressed.

Another characteristic in common between these disorders is feelings of low self-worth, inadequacy, or even worthlessness. It is not uncommon for individuals with either disorder to report automatic thoughts such as "I can't do this" or "I'll mess up" and also to report beliefs like "I'm inadequate." However, depression is more likely than SAD to include thoughts clustering around themes of hopelessness, worthlessness, and helplessness.

Both disorders may involve difficulties concentrating or sleeping. To properly distinguish them, it is important to ask individuals for the reasons behind the presence of these symptoms. For example, why is a person having trouble concentrating or falling asleep? In a depressed presentation, the person might report that they are ruminating about past failures or feeling guilty about being depressed. If the presentation is SAD, the individual might be more inclined to report worry about a previous or upcoming social event when trying to sleep.

As is the case for other anxiety disorders, SAD and depression are highly comorbid. Thus, it is likely that both disorders may be present for a given client.

1.5.5 Avoidant Personality Disorder

There is significant overlap between SAD and avoidant personality disorder (APD). DSM-5-TR defines APD as a pattern of social inhibition and sensitivity to negative evaluation (APA, 2022). Both disorders are characterized by this fear of negative evaluation, which leads to significant anxiety and avoidance of social situations. Even though fear and avoidance are present in both disorders, individuals desire social contact and interaction. Both disorders have onsets early in life. Degree of interpersonal sensitivity may be a useful way to distinguish these disorders. Whereas individuals with SAD are often sensitive about and fearful of being criticized, this quality appears to be more pervasive and marked in APD, with a unique feature of APD being emotional guardedness even with close others. People with SAD tend to feel safe with at least some close others, while people with APD may never become comfortable even with close others. Further, criteria can still be met for SAD even if concerns about being criticized are minimal. Some individuals present with concerns about embarrassing themselves or showing signs of anxiety rather than being criticized by others.

> SAD and APD share many features and may actually reflect the same underlying problem

1.5.6 Schizoid Personality Disorder

Schizoid personality disorder is characterized by detachment from and disinterest in social relationships, disinterest in sexual relationships, and few friends or relationships. Individuals with this disorder prefer to be alone and are virtually indifferent to praise or criticism from others. Schizoid personality disorder can appear similar to SAD because of the avoidance of social situations and the lack of close relationships (e.g., both conditions are often associated with avoidance of family gatherings, a lack of intimate relationships, and a tendency to be unmarried). However, there are a number of important distinctions between these disorders. The main distinction to bear in mind is that people with schizoid personality disorder are disinterested in social or intimate relationships, whereas people with SAD are often very interested in these relationships but are simply too anxious to be able to have them. Further, although many people with SAD have small social circles and are not in intimate relationships, a sizable proportion of them *are* in intimate relationships and report satisfaction with these relationships. Individuals with schizoid personality disorder are rarely involved in these relationships. Another distinction is the range of emotions experienced by individuals. Whereas individuals with schizoid personality disorder have more flat or constrained affect, individuals with SAD have an abundance of anxiety and nervous energy. This difference in affect is often very noticeable during a clinical interview.

1.6 Comorbidity

> Common comorbid conditions include anxiety disorders, depression, and substance use disorders

SAD is associated with an increased risk of a client having another disorder, including a depressive disorder, alcohol use disorder, or another anxiety disorder. Rates of individuals with SAD who have an additional current disorder are high, reaching 90% in some studies (Koyuncu et al., 2019). More specifically, people with SAD appear to have an increased risk of comorbid panic disorder, specific phobias, and depression. Individuals with SAD have been found to have a higher risk of alcohol dependence (Kushner et al., 2008) and cannabis dependence (Agosti et al., 2002) than those with other anxiety disorders. Individuals with SAD tend to report that they use alcohol and cannabis to cope with social situations (Buckner et al., 2012). These higher rates of comorbidity can have an impact on severity of SAD as well as treatment outcome. Clients with SAD who also had an additional diagnosis of depression were found to have a longer duration of SAD symptoms and more severe impairment both before and after treatment than those with a sole diagnosis of SAD (Erwin et al., 2002), though trajectories of change in CBT appear to be similar between individuals with SAD and SAD plus depression (LeMoult et al., 2014). It is likely that the presence of any comorbid disorder will have negative implications for the severity and prognosis of SAD.

1.7 Diagnostic Procedures and Documentation

Accurate diagnosis of SAD is important for selecting an appropriate treatment. Given that the experience of SAD is heterogeneous across individuals, it is also useful to assess ideographic aspects of the presentation, including the severity of an individual's presentation, the presence of particular salient features (e.g., safety behaviors), and the extent to which symptoms change as a result of treatment. A host of measures exist for assessing these domains, including interviewer-administered scales, self-report questionnaires, and behavioral assessments.

It is also important to consider a number of nonspecific factors when assessing symptoms of SAD. An assessment, itself, is a social interaction and may be highly anxiety provoking for someone with SAD. Forming a therapeutic alliance and emphasizing the nonjudgmental and confidential nature of the interview will help set the stage for individuals to share personal information that they may typically conceal. It may not be useful to use small talk as a way of connecting if this is a feared task for the individual, challenging clinicians to find other ways of connecting with inhibited clients. Combining open-ended questions with examples that the individual can endorse may help collect both idiosyncratic information, but also normalize common examples of feared situations, concerns, or triggers. It can also be useful to flexibly shift between structured or semistructured interviews and self-report tasks, relieving the potential burden of the individual feeling like the center of attention.

Attention to cultural and diversity considerations is important in assessment. It is important to consider cultural norms (e.g., How concerning is embarrassment within the individual's family or culture? Is eye contact valued or discouraged? What are the person's cultural beliefs about independence?), level of acculturation, experiences of discrimination, whether avoidance or self-concealment is actually protective for racialized or minoritized individuals (e.g., it may be objectively dangerous to reveal one's nonbinary or trans status within certain majority groups), and whether distress from social anxiety arises from a mismatch of personal and cultural norms. For example, an individual from a collectivist culture who finds themselves in an individualistic culture may suddenly find their level of social anxiety and withdrawal to be problematic according to the broader cultural norms. It is also useful for clinicians to reflect on their own cultural influences and how these might affect the assessment. Simple questions like "Is there anything from your cultural/religious/family background that you'd like me to consider?" can open up fruitful conversations about the context in which we need to understand a person's symptoms.

> **Individuals with SAD from marginalized groups may have experienced discrimination and prejudice**

1.7.1 Interviewer-Administered Measures

Diagnostic Assessment Research Tool
The Diagnostic Assessment Research Tool (DART; McCabe et al., 2021) is a semistructured, open-access, modular interview that assesses a range of DSM-5-TR disorders. Relevant modules (e.g., SAD, other anxiety disorders, depressive disorders, substance use disorders) can be used to gather information about symptoms in a consistent and reliable fashion. Initial psychometrics of the DART suggest that it has good interrater agreement and strong convergent and discriminant validity for the SAD module (as well as the majority of diagnostic categories assessed). Given that the DART is widely available at no cost and only relevant modules can be selected for administration, it is a cost-effective and efficient tool for clinicians when assessing the diagnostic status of SAD and related comorbidities.

Liebowitz Social Anxiety Scale

The Liebowitz Social Anxiety Scale (LSAS; Liebowitz, 1987) is a 24-item clinician-rated scale designed to assess the severity of a range of social and performance concerns. Respondents are asked about both fear and avoidance of a series of situations over the past week, yielding total fear and avoidance scores as well as a number of subscale scores (fear of social interaction, fear of performance, total fear, avoidance of social interaction, avoidance of performance, and total avoidance). The LSAS appears to be a reliable measure with good treatment sensitivity (Heimberg et al., 1999) and has been translated into languages other than English and used with numerous minority populations. This measure is useful to include in a pre- and posttreatment assessment battery as it only takes about 20 minutes to complete and provides a helpful addition to self-reported symptom measures. The LSAS has also been validated in a self-report format (e.g., Rytwinski et al., 2009).

Brief Social Phobia Scale

The Brief Social Phobia Scale (BSPS; Davidson et al., 1991) is an 18-item interviewer-rated scale designed to assess the severity of symptoms of SAD. Similar to the LSAS, respondents are asked to rate both fear and avoidance of a number of social situations over the past week. These measures differ in that the BSPS inquires about fewer situations (seven) than the LSAS, but also asks about physiological symptoms that may occur in social situations. The situations assessed include speaking in front of others, talking to people in authority, talking to strangers, being embarrassed or humiliated, being criticized, social gatherings, and doing something while being watched. It is a briefer measure than the LSAS and the DART, only taking 5 to 15 minutes to administer, but its authors suggest using it in conjunction with another interview-based measure for thoroughness. Internal consistency for this interview is adequate, and it has demonstrated good validity and treatment sensitivity. It appears that the fear and avoidance subscales of this measure are psychometrically stronger than the physiological subscale, suggesting that these may be the subscales to focus on when assessing treatment outcome (Davidson et al., 1997).

1.7.2 Self-Report Severity Measures

Social Phobia Inventory

> A brief version of the SPIN has been developed

The Social Phobia Inventory (SPIN; Connor et al., 2000) is a 17-item self-report measure assessing how much a series of symptoms of social anxiety bother the respondent. Items fall into three subscales including fear, avoidance, and physiological arousal. Individuals complete the SPIN based on the previous week, making this a useful measure to assess week-to-week progress during treatment for SAD. Another appealing characteristic of the SPIN is its brevity. It takes several minutes to complete, allowing the client to quickly complete it at the beginning of a treatment session. The psychometric properties of the SPIN are very good (Antony, Coons et al., 2006; Connor et al.,

2000), and it has been translated into multiple languages. The total score demonstrates excellent internal consistency, and correlations with interviewer measures of SAD suggest it has good convergent validity. The authors of the SPIN suggest that a cutoff score of 19 (out of a possible 68) is useful in discriminating those with SAD and those without at an accuracy rate of 79%, though other authors suggest a higher cutoff score of 30 (e.g., Moscovitch et al., 2011).

Ryerson Social Anxiety Scales

The Ryerson Social Anxiety Scales (Rogojanski et al., 2019) is a self-report measure that assesses both the breadth of situations that trigger social anxiety as well as the degree of distress and impairment experienced in these situations (see Appendix 1). Respondents indicate level of fear and anxiety for 23 social situations and then rate the distress and impairment associated with these situations. Psychometric studies suggest this is a reliable and valid tool across both nonclinical (Lenton-Brym et al., 2020) and clinical (Tsekova et al., 2021) samples.

Social Phobia Scale

The Social Phobia Scale (SPS; Mattick & Clarke, 1998) is a 20-item self-report scale focusing on anxiety while being observed by others. Respondents rate how much each situation would bother them on a scale from *not at all* to *extremely true of me*. Situations include activities such as using public toilets, entering rooms where others are seated, fainting or being ill in front of others, and eating or drinking in front of others. This is also a brief measure, taking only minutes to complete. This feature makes the SPS a popular measure to use in treatment studies or to monitor weekly progress in treatment. The SPS demonstrates excellent reliability. Even though there are items on the SPS that seem related to agoraphobic concerns, individuals with SAD score higher on this scale than do those with agoraphobia. The SPS has been well studied and appears to demonstrate strong psychometric properties including treatment sensitivity (see Ashbaugh et al., 2020, for a review).

Social Interaction Anxiety Scale

The Social Interaction Anxiety Scale (Mattick & Clarke, 1998) self-report measure was designed in conjunction with the SPS and assesses fears of interacting with others. Sample items include concerns about talking with others, mixing at parties, and saying something embarrassing when talking. It is also 20 items and therefore is brief and easy for clients to complete. As with the SPS, it also demonstrates strong psychometric properties and studies suggest that the two measures, though related, are assessing different constructs (see Ashbaugh et al., 2020, for a review).

Negative Self-Portrayal Scale

The Negative Self-Portrayal Scale (Moscovitch & Huyder, 2011) self-report measure assesses self-perceived deficits that may be revealed and judged by others in a social situation. The items are 27 negative self-attributes that cluster into three factors: concerns about appearing socially incompetent, physically unattractive, or visibly anxious. The Negative Self-Portrayal Scale is brief and easy for individuals to complete and provides the therapist with ideas about aspects of self that the person is likely concealing in social situations. The Negative Self-Portrayal Scale has good psychometric properties (Moscovitch et al., 2015).

1.7.3 Behavioral Approach Tests

A Behavioral Approach Test (BAT) involves instructing a client to enter a feared situation or engage in a feared activity and monitoring their responses. Using behavioral assessment strategies can provide important information not provided by interviews or self-report alone. For example, a client with a tendency to minimize fears may report little or no avoidance of a particular situation, but then may freeze when in the actual situation. BATs can also be used to assess treatment outcome. A change in performance on a behavioral task provides real-world information about the effectiveness of treatment.

A commonly used BAT for SAD involves asking a client to give a speech in front of another person, a small audience, or a video camera. This situation is often used because public speaking is one of the most common fears that adults report, suggesting that it is likely to be anxiety provoking for most individuals, especially those with a diagnosis of SAD. Other potential BATs include having the individual engage in a spontaneous conversation or talk about themselves to others. Although it is sometimes useful to have all participants engage in a consistent BAT for the purpose of research, it is typically more appropriate to use individually tailored BATs in clinical practice, selecting situations that are most relevant to the individual's phobia and treatment goals.

When designing a BAT, the clinician and client should identify a highly feared situation (ideally, one of the most feared situations) and then have the client enter that situation both before and after treatment (and perhaps several times during the course of treatment). During the BAT, clients should provide subjective fear ratings to communicate their distress, using a scale ranging from 0 (*no fear at all*) to 100 (*as much fear as can be imagined*). In addition to subjective fear ratings, other indicators of fear can be useful as well, including whether the client can complete the BAT and how long they spend in the situation.

1.7.4 Assessing Suitability for Treatment

As clinicians, we often assume that people are ready to engage in whatever treatment we have to offer when they present in a clinical setting. We also know that CBT is an effective treatment for SAD, so we may assume that this approach is always a good match for a client who presents to us with this problem. However, full benefit from a treatment like CBT depends on the active participation of clients. Clients have to be willing to "buy into" the cognitive behavioral model of social anxiety and practice the CBT techniques. Homework is an important part of successful CBT, requiring the client to not only attend appointments, but also to practice using techniques and completing exercises between sessions. However, many clients are not fully ready to commit to CBT or may be ambivalent about engaging in treatment. It is helpful to know whether clients are ready to begin active treatment, almost ready, or not likely to benefit from treatment at the current time. Knowing this information is useful not only for the clinician (i.e., it reduces the amount of time and frustration spent with clients who are not ready), but also for the client who might feel frustrated or hopeless about trying and "failing" a therapy that they were not ready to undertake. For these reasons, it can be helpful to assess suitability and readiness for CBT.

To briefly assess suitability for CBT for SAD, consider the following areas. First, what is the client's reaction to the CBT model? Do they understand the detrimental role that avoidance and safety behaviors play in maintaining anxiety? Can they label their feared predictions in social situations? Are they willing to experience temporary increases in anxiety and fear in order to eventually feel more comfortable in social situations?

Furthermore, do clients show interest in the structure and style of CBT? CBT for social anxiety is present focused, so clients who are looking to examine the developmental or unconscious roots of their anxiety may not enjoy a problem-focused approach such as CBT. Do clients indicate a willingness to complete homework? Do they understand the crucial role that between-session work has on treatment outcome? It is useful to ask about previous attempts at therapy, including CBT and other techniques. How did the client react to previous therapies? Were they able to do the work required by previous therapists? Clinicians could also investigate the relative strength of the client's fear of engaging in treatment (e.g., completing experiments, confronting anxiety) versus the costs and frustrations of living with anxiety.

2

Psychological Approaches to Understanding SAD

There are a number of psychological models and theories of the development and maintenance of SAD. Each model is associated with particular nuances in the treatment of SAD, but together they provide a foundation for the conceptualization and treatment of SAD.

2.1 Clark and Wells's Cognitive Models (1995, 2001)

Clark and Wells (1995) proposed a cognitive model of SAD based on their clinical observations and research, which Clark updated in 2001. Their model begins with the assumption that people with SAD are invested in making a positive impression on others but are insecure about their ability to do so. These insecurities likely arise from distorted beliefs that people with SAD hold about themselves. Common negative beliefs in SAD include "I'm stupid" or "I'm boring." People with SAD also hold negative assumptions about themselves and others (e.g., "If I'm quiet people will think I'm boring" and "If people see my anxiety, they'll think I'm stupid") and rigid rules about how they should behave in social situations (e.g., "I should never show signs of anxiety" or "I should always have something interesting to say"). Box 1 provides additional examples of negative beliefs, assumptions, and rules often associated with SAD. Clearly, holding strong and negative ideas such as these about oneself and about how one should perform in social situations can leave a person vulnerable to experiencing high levels of anxiety in these situations.

> Cognitive models hypothesize that people with SAD engage in problematic self-focused attention

A central tenet of this model is people with SAD tend to focus on *themselves* in social situations rather than attending to what others are saying and doing. In some ways, this is contradictory to what we might expect – we might assume that people with SAD would be constantly monitoring how others are reacting to them and whether others seem to like them, accept them, and so forth. However, Clark and Wells suggest that attention becomes self-focused, to the point that the individual might ignore or miss important social cues. Self-focused attention is promoted by the increase in physiological symptoms a person experiences when anticipating or entering a social situation. In other words, as the person becomes more anxious, bodily sensations intensify, and these sensations cause a shift in attention to oneself and one's body. The ultimate result of self-focused attention is an increased feeling of conspicuousness. All of a sudden, the person feels like they are "on stage" or the center of attention. Individuals with SAD may even see themselves as if they are watching themselves on television and have negative self-images. One client reported feeling so hot and sweaty that they had an image of themself with a bright red and sweaty face "like a tomato." In reality, this may not have been the true state of affairs but such an impression served to exacerbate anxiety and reduce the person's ability to attend to social feedback. Thus, a core feature of this model is to shift self-focused attention to externally focused attention, which helps explain improvements in social anxiety across time (Mörtberg et al., 2015).

> **Box 1**
> **Examples of Beliefs, Assumptions, and Rules in Social Anxiety Disorder**
>
> **Beliefs**
> - I'm stupid
> - I'm boring
> - I'm weird, odd, or different
>
> **Assumptions**
> - If I make a mistake, others will think I'm stupid
> - If other people notice my anxiety, they'll think I'm weird
> - If one person doesn't like me, no one will like me
>
> **Rules**
> - Everyone should like me
> - I should never show that I'm nervous
> - I should always look "perfect"
> - I should always sound intelligent and interesting

The host of negative beliefs people with SAD hold may also cause them to behave differently than nonanxious people in stressful situations. Clark and Wells call some of these behaviors "safety behaviors." Safety behaviors are those that help the person avoid a feared catastrophe and feel safer in a particular situation. Examples of safety behaviors can be found in Box 2.

Another common strategy used by people with SAD is avoidance of a stressful situation. Both safety behaviors and avoidance are completely understandable. Who would want to put themselves in a highly stressful situation? However, Clark and Wells point out that avoidance and safety behaviors lead to a number of problems. First, some safety behaviors may actually exacerbate feared bodily sensations. For example, wearing an extra jacket to hide any sweating actually makes a person warmer and therefore more likely to sweat. Another problem associated with avoidance and safety behaviors is the prevention of any opportunity to learn that negative outcomes typically do not occur. For example, by not ever giving a speech, a person can never

People with SAD often use safety behaviors to reduce anxiety or protect themselves from perceived social danger

learn that they may be perfectly capable of public speaking or that the audience is much less likely to be critical or dismissing than anticipated. Using safety behaviors gives the person a ready-made excuse for why a catastrophe did not happen. A third problem is that safety and avoidance behaviors contain their own messages to others that may be more damaging than the person's original feared outcome. For example, if a person is afraid of not having anything to say in a conversation, they may rehearse questions and answers in their head while the other person talks (a safety behavior). Although this behavior is intended to *help* the conversation, it may actually *hurt* the conversation. This individual may come off as disinterested, aloof, or disengaged from the conversation, actually *increasing* their chance of being socially "rejected." Research supports the idea that safety behaviors can explain impaired performance (Rowa et al., 2015) and contribute to feelings of inauthenticity (Plasencia et al., 2016).

Box 2
Examples of Safety Behaviors in Social Anxiety Disorder

- Overly rehearse what I'm going to say in a conversation; prepare questions in advance
- Keep my camera off on a video call
- Sit on my hands so people can't see them shaking
- Sit in the back row of a class or in the corner of the meeting room
- Wear a turtleneck sweater to hide blushing and splotches on my neck and chest
- Take on a "role" at a social event to prevent having to make small talk
- Memorize my speech
- Wear cool clothes or a jacket over my shirt to hide any sweating
- Eat in a dimly lit restaurant to prevent people from noticing my blushing
- Grip my water bottle very tightly to prevent hands from shaking
- Always be perfectly dressed and made up before going out

Avoidance also can be associated with negative consequences. By repeatedly declining social invitations, the person's friends may grow tired of continually asking but being rejected. By repeatedly avoiding things like meetings, a person may be putting themself in jeopardy of being fired or not considered for promotions. Safety behaviors and avoidance are important components of a feedback cycle that contributes to the maintenance of negative beliefs about the self and negative predictions about what will happen if the person were to enter a feared situation. With these negative beliefs and predications intact and perhaps strengthened, anxiety symptoms are maintained. While both avoidance and safety behaviors are important treatment targets arising from the Clark and Wells model, Clark's 2001 update places more emphasis on safety behaviors as the crucial target behavior that maintains SAD.

The final piece of Clark and Wells's model involves the notion that negative beliefs, rules, and predictions do not just occur when the person is in the feared situation. Indeed, negative processing is theorized to occur before the person even enters a feared situation ("anticipatory processing"). The person may review all the terrible things that could happen, how they may screw up, and how badly things have gone in the past. This type of processing will either cause the person to completely avoid the situation, or to enter the situation in a state where they are already in a self-focused, negative mindset. After making it through a difficult situation, people with SAD also tend to review how things went (what Clark and Wells refer to as the "postmortem"). Unfortunately, for all the reasons described earlier, the situation may not have gone well or the person with SAD may have disregarded any positive or neutral feedback, meaning that the postmortem review will only serve to consolidate negative beliefs. Indeed, research suggests that postevent processing contributes to the cycle of avoidance in SAD (Rowa et al., 2016) and is more problematic in SAD than other anxiety disorders (Perera et al., 2016).

2.2 Rapee and Heimberg's Cognitive Behavioral Models (1997, 2010, 2014)

Rapee and Heimberg (1997) have also described a cognitive behavioral model of SAD (with updates in 2010 and 2014) that shares many features with Clark and Wells's model but also contains some unique ideas. Both models share the notion that people with SAD hold negative beliefs about themselves and are likely to predict that bad things will happen in stressful situations. Further, the occurrence of negative evaluation by others is seen as being "catastrophic," making it a highly undesirable outcome. Both models discuss the unhelpful nature of avoidance and subtle avoidance (or safety behaviors), suggesting that they can actually contribute to worse outcomes even though they are used to help a person get through a stressful situation. Both models emphasize the importance of postevent processing in SAD, with this ruminative process contributing to progressively more negative and distorted perceptions of a social event and one's responsibility for the event over time.

The Rapee and Heimberg models explicitly discuss the notion that the perceived threat in SAD is the reaction of an "audience." By audience, they are referring to any person who may perceive or notice an individual. Thus, if there is no perceived audience, social anxiety is unlikely to exist. However, because most social or performance situations include at least a possible audience, the person with SAD is likely to feel anxious in many social situations. An audience can even exist when no one is present; the individual with SAD may anticipate an audience ahead of a social interaction. Individuals with SAD perceive the audience as having high standards that are difficult to reach and tend to be afraid of both negative and positive evaluation from the audience. As a result of being concerned about an audience reaction, people with SAD create or access a mental representation of how they look or appear to this audience. This mental representation is influenced by a number of factors including a self-image from memory, pictures, physical symptoms, and

> People with SAD believe that others hold unreasonably high expectations of them

social feedback. This mental image of oneself is often distorted. For example, people with SAD often rate their performance as poor, even if this is not objectively true. Rapee and Heimberg argue that anxiety may sometimes interfere with performance, leading to objective evidence that one is "incapable" or a "failure."

The Rapee and Heimberg models emphasize the importance of negative imagery in SAD. Individuals with SAD experience imagery before, during, and after social situations that also influences their mental representation of self. This imagery tends to be distorted, encouraging ongoing negative expectations of the audience's reaction to them and potentially disrupting social performance.

Not only do people with SAD monitor their mental representation of themselves, but they also pay a great deal of attention to looking for sources of "threat." Threat usually comes in the form of being negatively evaluated by others, so the person with SAD looks externally for signs of rejection, disinterest, or embarrassment. Unfortunately, it is often hard to tell what others are thinking, and it is rare to receive straightforward feedback about one's

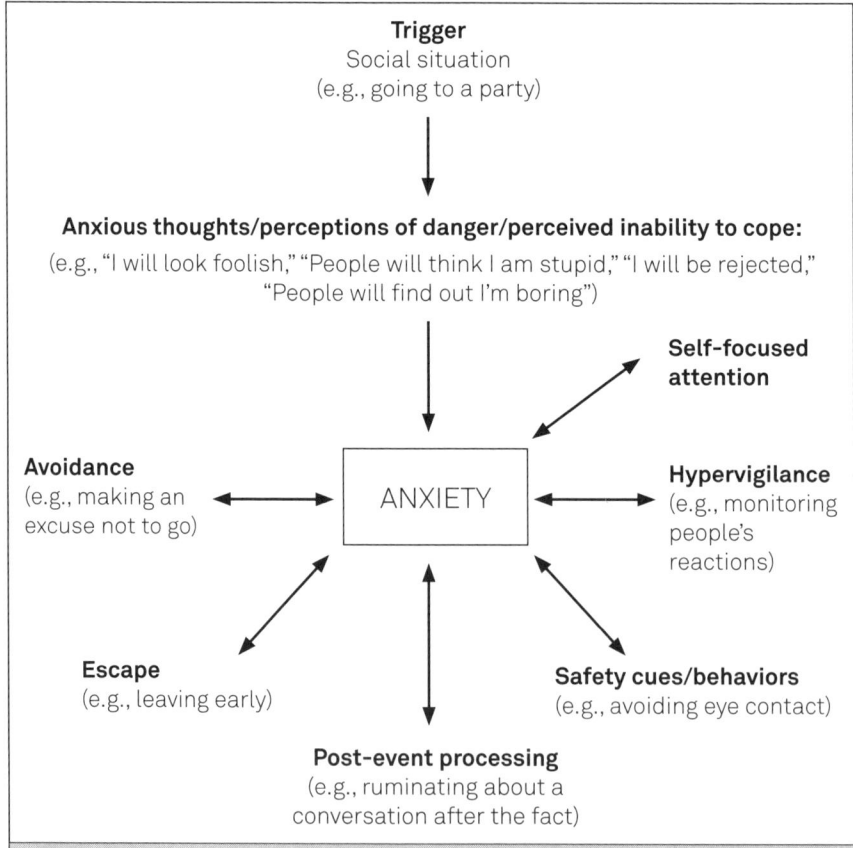

Figure 1
Generic cognitive behavioral model of SAD. Reprinted with permission from McConnell et al., 2017.

performance (e.g., "I wasn't paying attention in the meeting because I was thinking about my children, not because you were boring"). Therefore, it is easy to distort or twist social information to be consistent with one's fears. Someone yawning during a talk is easily interpreted as a sign of the speaker being boring, and the person yawning is easily picked out of a crowd of neutral faces when a great deal of attention is allocated to signs of threat. In this model, the individual's excessive monitoring oscillates between internal cues (i.e., self-focused attention) and external threats.

Similar across both models is the notion that feedback loops exist to maintain social anxiety and maintain distorted predictions and beliefs about self and others. See Figure 1 for a visual representation of the feedback loops. For example, perceptions of oneself as awkward or unable to carry on a conversation will lead to heightened anxiety when there is a perceived audience. This heightened anxiety leads to an increase in bodily sensations, which strengthens one's self-perceptions of being awkward and appearing anxious. As a result, the individual may be inclined to leave the stressful situation, or to avoid it altogether, not allowing them to test out their assumptions of what would happen if they stayed even though they are anxious.

2.3 Hofmann and Aderka's Integrated Cognitive Behavioral Models (2007, 2021)

Hofmann (2007) developed an integrated CBT model of SAD (which was updated by Aderka and Hofmann in 2021) that is influenced by Clark and Wells's original model but also integrates emotional processes and heavily emphasizes the importance of an ideographic conceptualization of each client's symptoms. This model notes that people with SAD perceive high (or ambiguous) social standards but low social abilities. As mentioned earlier, there is no clear evidence that individuals with SAD have uniform deficits in social skills, but this perception creates apprehension when approaching any social situation or interaction with a fear that one is not able to perform at the expected level. Individuals with SAD experience elevated self-focused attention, which triggers or enhances negative thoughts about oneself ("I'm so weird"), fears that the cost of poor social performance is high ("It will be humiliating if I don't text something witty back"), and that they have no control over their emotions and others will notice this ("I can't stop myself from stuttering and everyone will notice"). Hofmann's original emphasis on emotional control has been extended to other emotional processes, namely poor ability to label and differentiate emotions, an unwillingness to experience negative internal states including emotions, and poor emotion regulation. These emotional processes are all thought to contribute to concerns about poor emotional control. Similar to the models described above, individuals with SAD use avoidance and safety behaviors to manage these concerns, leading to postevent rumination (the "postmortem"), and contributing to the maintenance of anxiety in the ways noted earlier.

2.4 Moscovitch's Model (2009)

Another reconceptualization of the CBT models above is Moscovitch's model in which the feared targets in SAD are not the social situations themselves but rather what the individual with SAD fears they will reveal about themselves in a particular situation. These self-portrayal concerns include concerns about having flawed social skills, personality, physical appearance, and noticeable signs of anxiety. The fear of revealing these negative self-attributes drives avoidance and safety-behavior use, including individuals trying to conceal perceived flaws. Differences in the amount and intensity of each of these four areas of concern will vary across individuals with SAD, suggesting the importance of a personalized conceptualization in understanding anxiety and associated safety behaviors. This model is one of the first to explicitly incorporate the "self" into a model of SAD (see also Stopa, 2009) and suggests that treatment should focus less about avoided *situations* and more about designing exercises for someone to experiment with revealing feared aspects of self across any relevant situation. Research supports the notion that individuals with SAD have higher self-portrayal concerns than individuals with other anxiety disorders, and that these concerns predict the use of safety behaviors (Moscovitch et al., 2013).

A summary of the key points from all the CBT models is provided in Box 3.

Box 3
Summary of Key Points From CBT Models of Social Anxiety Disorder

- People with SAD want to make a good impression on others
- They hold negative beliefs about themselves and their ability to perform in social situations
- They worry about negative evaluation from others
- They fear that they will not be able to cope in social situations
- When in social situations, people with SAD focus on themselves and see themselves as if they are watching themselves on television
- These self-images tend to be biased and inaccurate
- Focusing on themselves does not allow people with SAD to fully participate in the social situation
- People with SAD either avoid situations or use safety behaviors in feared situations
- Safety behaviors and avoidance do not allow the person to learn that fears may not actually come true
- Safety behaviors may create unintended negative side effects
- Negative thinking about social situations occurs before, during, and after the situation

2.5 Negative Learning Experiences and Social Anxiety

Models that include negative learning experiences in the etiology of fear have applications for understanding the development of SAD. Rachman (1977) highlighted three pathways to the development of fears. These pathways include (1) *direct conditioning*, which refers to a stimulus becoming associated with a fear reaction though a traumatic experience, (2) *vicarious acquisition*, which involves witnessing someone else have a fearful reaction or upsetting social experience, and (3) *informational pathways*, which involve learning that a particular stimulus (i.e., social situations) is dangerous through information transmitted by others (e.g., on social media, during conversations, while reading).

There is some evidence for the presence of these pathways to fear in SAD. For example, retrospective reports of individuals with SAD suggest that they experienced more teasing in childhood than did individuals with obsessive compulsive disorder or panic disorder (McCabe et al., 2003), reports of severe bullying during childhood were related to a higher prevalence of SAD in clients presenting to an outpatient depression clinic (Gladstone et al., 2006), and reports of being frequently teased during childhood were related to scores on measures of social anxiety in college students (Roth et al., 2002). Further, several studies have found that socially anxious individuals are often raised by socially isolated parents, and that parents may hold these children and adolescents back from social experiences (e.g., Bögels et al., 2001). This kind of evidence can be construed as potential sources of both vicarious acquisition (e.g., watching a parent act in an anxious, withdrawn manner) and/or informational learning (e.g., being instructed by anxious parents that social outings are dangerous; being exposed to messages through social media regarding the importance of meeting impossibly high social standards).

> People with SAD have often experienced difficult social events in their past

Although there is some evidence suggesting that negative learning experiences may play a role in the development of SAD, they cannot fully explain how SAD develops. Many people with SAD cannot recall traumatic experiences and grew up in socially supportive environments. Similarly, many people who do not develop symptoms of SAD can recall adverse childhood experiences like being teased. Therefore, negative learning experiences are just one potential pathway to the development of this disorder.

2.6 Temperamental Bases of SAD

Some authors have been interested in the temperamental and developmental precursors to SAD. Are some people simply born with SAD? The answer to this appears to be that some people are born with a *vulnerability* to developing SAD. No one gene can explain the development of SAD – anxiety disorders are too complex to be controlled by single genes. Similarly, not every child born to a parent with SAD will also develop this disorder and not every individual with SAD has an afflicted parent, though SAD tends to aggregate

> Behavioral inhibition in infancy is predictive of later developing an anxiety disorder, such as SAD

within families, suggesting some genetic component as well as environmental influences. The temperamental vulnerability most linked with social anxiety is called *behavioral inhibition*. Behavioral inhibition involves a tendency to overreact to novel environmental stimuli in social domains and is thought to have a genetic basis. In other words, a child demonstrating behavioral inhibition will show physiological reactivity, shyness, and possible withdrawal when faced with a new situation (e.g., clinging to one's parent when meeting a new adult). Studies have found a relationship between behavioral inhibition in childhood and the development of social anxiety (Hirshfeld-Becker et al., 2014). This link is especially strong for children whose signs of inhibition were consistent across multiple testing situations (i.e., when behavioral inhibition appears in a number of situations, not just in isolated incidents).

Although behavioral inhibition appears to be fairly stable across time, especially among individuals with extreme levels of behavioral inhibition, there is some variability in this construct over time. Some authors have argued that this suggests that family and peer interactions also influence levels of social anxiety (Neal & Edelmann, 2003). Indeed, the interaction of a temperamental style with environment is an intuitively meaningful way to understand the development of SAD. An inhibited child will be more likely to "pull" for overprotective behaviors from their parent, which then reduces the child's opportunities to get used to novel situations, thus strengthening their inhibition. Studies suggest that parents of inhibited and shy children may be more overprotective, intrusive, insensitive, and shaming (Hudson & Rapee, 2001). As children begin to interact with peers, research suggests that initial shyness or passivity is tolerated until adolescence, but then results in rejection (Blöte & Westenberg, 2007), which is associated with later social anxiety (Chiu et al., 2021).

2.7 Implications for Treatment

The models described in this chapter have implications for the treatment of SAD. Cognitive behavioral treatments focus on helping a person to gain a more realistic perspective on their negative beliefs and predictions. Clients are asked to consider the evidence for their anxious beliefs and to actively test their assumptions in order to come to realistic conclusions about the likely outcome of social events. CBT also focuses on changing the coping strategies used by people with SAD. The use of avoidance and safety behaviors are gradually reduced, allowing the person to find out what actually happens in these situations and to learn to cope with any untoward outcomes or high levels of anxiety. Techniques such as video feedback may be used to help pull the person's focus of attention from *internal* cues to *external* social cues (e.g., Laposa & Rector, 2023; Orr & Moscovitch, 2010). Given the relationships among thoughts, emotions, and coping strategies, a focus on any one of these areas should help shift the entire system.

3

Diagnosis and Treatment Indications

This chapter provides the clinician with a framework for understanding a client's SAD, and for selecting an appropriate course of treatment. It begins with a discussion of key features to be assessed, followed by an overview of effective treatment strategies, and guidelines for how to use information from the assessment to plan for treatment.

3.1 Key Features to Be Assessed

Key features that should be assessed include situational triggers, physical features, cognitive features, distressing images, avoidance strategies, safety behaviors, anxiety sensitivity, social skills, environmental factors, cultural factors, comorbidity, and degree of impairment. The extent to which these various features are present in any given client will influence the types of strategies that are used, and the ways in which they are implemented. This discussion also includes recommended instruments that can be used to aid assessment.

3.1.1 Situational Triggers

Many forms of CBT focus on being able to identify situations that trigger an individual's fear. In the case of SAD, these include performance situations in which an individual might be the center of attention (e.g., public speaking), as well as interpersonal or social interaction situations (e.g., dating, meeting strangers). In collaboration with the client, the clinician should generate a comprehensive list of the client's feared situations that can be used for exposure practices.

Scales that can be useful for generating a list of situational triggers include self-report measures such as the Ryerson Social Anxiety Scales (Rogojanski et al., 2019), Social Phobia Inventory (Connor et al., 2000), Social Phobia Scale (Mattick & Clarke, 1998), and Social Interaction Anxiety Inventory (Mattick & Clarke, 1998), as well as clinician-administered skills such as the BSPS (Davidson et al., 1991) and LSAS (Liebowitz, 1987). Chapter 1 includes detailed descriptions of these scales.

3.1.2 Physical Features

Individuals with SAD may overestimate the extent to which their physical symptoms are noticeable to others

People with SAD often experience panic attacks in the presence of the situations that they fear. Symptoms of autonomic arousal (e.g., increased heart rate) are particularly common in performance-related fears. Individuals with SAD tend to be most concerned about physical sensations that might be noticeable to others, such as blushing, shaking, and sweating. However, it is important to note that a person's beliefs about the intensity of these symptoms are not necessarily related to the actual intensity of these symptoms. For individuals who are concerned about experiencing particular physical symptoms, it may be useful to include treatment strategies that target the fear of sensations (see Section 3.1.7, on anxiety sensitivity).

3.1.3 Cognitive Features

It's useful to identify the specific predictions that the client is making with respect to social situations

An assessment of anxiety-provoking thoughts and predictions is important in planning for a course of CBT. Chapter 2 (Box 1) includes examples of beliefs, assumptions, and rules that often contribute to social anxiety. Questions that may be useful for assessing the cognitive features of social anxiety include:

- What do you imagine will happen when you _____ (name situation)?
- What might occur if people were to notice your _____ (name symptom)?
- What might people think of you if you were to _____ (name feared outcome)?
- What is your most feared outcome when you think about doing _____ (name situation)?
- What would be so bad about doing _____ in front of others?
- What would be so bad about people thinking _____ about you?
- What would it mean about you if others were to think _____ about you?
- Do you fear that others will think you are stupid? Incompetent? Boring? Rude? Anxious? Weak? Silly? Foolish?

Note that each of these questions is designed to assess an anxiety-provoking belief about something that might happen in the future in a social or performance situation (e.g., "what might happen if you were to make a mistake in front of others?"), or to assess the client's beliefs about the meaning of possible events (e.g., "what would it mean about if you were to blush in front of others?"). A thorough assessment of the cognitive features of SAD should occur before the start of treatment, though the process should continue throughout therapy as well. To gather information about feared self-attributes that the person is afraid of revealing, the Negative Self-Portrayal Scale (Moscovitch et al., 2015) may be used.

The content of cognitive features of SAD may differ across cultures and within particular minoritized groups. For example, individuals with *taijin kyofusho* worry about offending others and therefore questions to assess cognitive features should specifically ask about how and why a perceived offense has taken place.

3.1.4 Imagery

Individuals with SAD often experience negative mental images while in anxiety-provoking situations. These images tend to be distorted and from an observer's perspective. For example, one of our clients shared a recurrent image of themselves as "quaking in the background" of a social situation. It is important to ask about meaningful mental images, including content, sensory details, and the meaning individuals give to their images. Although the presence of imagery should be universally assessed, imagery may be more prevalent and self-focused in Western cultures. For example, as compared to Western cultures, individuals in Korea were found to report fewer images than those from Western cultures and content that includes other people rather than the self (Suh et al., 2020).

3.1.5 Avoidance Strategies

The most obvious forms of avoidance in SAD include refusal to enter a feared situation (e.g., avoiding taking courses that involve making a presentation) and escape from a feared situation shortly after entering (e.g., leaving a party after 15 minutes). A list of situations that are avoided is important for assessing the severity of SAD and for developing appropriate exposure exercises. In most cases, the list of avoided situations will be similar to the list of situational triggers for social anxiety as discussed in Section 3.1.1. The assessment tools mentioned in that section are all useful for developing a list of avoided situations.

Most people with SAD will also use more subtle avoidance strategies to manage the intensity of their anxiety and fear when in social situations, and to prevent their feared consequences from occurring. These strategies are discussed in Section 3.1.6.

Subtle avoidance strategies such as distraction are commonly used by people with SAD

3.1.6 Safety Behaviors

Safety behaviors are behaviors that individuals use to protect themselves from feeling overly anxious or to prevent their feared consequences from actually occurring. One subtype of safety behaviors is self-concealment strategies; an attempt to hide a perceived flaw about oneself. Examples of safety behaviors can be found in Box 2.

There is evidence that, among individuals with SAD, safety behaviors contribute to impairment in social performance (Rowa et al., 2015; Stangier et al., 2006), and that overuse of safety behaviors can interfere with the outcome of psychological treatment for SAD (see Piccirillo et al., 2016 for a review). Therefore, reduction of safety behaviors is an important goal of treatment. The Subtle Avoidance Frequency Examination (Cuming et al., 2009) and the Social Behaviours Questionnaire (Mörtberg et al., 2007) are examples of scales designed to measure safety behaviors in this population.

3.1.7 Anxiety Sensitivity

> People with SAD often have elevated anxiety over experiencing symptoms of arousal and fear

Anxiety sensitivity refers to anxiety over experiencing physical symptoms of anxiety, such as elevated heart rate, dizziness, shaking, shortness of breath. People with SAD tend to be particularly concerned about experiencing observable anxiety reactions (e.g., blushing, shaking, sweating), compared to people with other anxiety disorders. Unlike individuals with panic disorder who are fearful of experiencing physical sensations of arousal across a wide range of situations, people with SAD are generally more likely to fear these sensations only in social or performance-related situations.

The most extensively studied measure for assessing anxiety sensitivity is the Anxiety Sensitivity Index (Peterson & Reiss, 1993). There are a number of unofficial revisions of the Anxiety Sensitivity Index available, the most popular of which is the Anxiety Sensitivity Index-3 (Taylor et al., 2007).

3.1.8 Social Skills

> Many people with this disorder have intact social skills and deficits are often secondary to the use of safety behaviors

In many cases, cognitive behavioral treatment assumes that the main problem in SAD is an individual's belief that they are likely to behave in a socially unacceptable way and their use of safety behaviors, rather than a true impairment in social skills. For individuals with social skills deficits, treatment is effective regardless of whether social skills are targeted directly, though including social-skills training may lead to better outcomes (e.g., Beidel et al., 2014). For clients with severe social skills deficits (including individuals with autism spectrum disorder; e.g., Bemmer et al., 2021), it may be particularly helpful to include social-skills training as a component of treatment, after ensuring that any skills deficits are not related to ongoing use of safety behaviors. In clinical settings, social skills impairment is typically assessed through behavioral observation and information derived from the clinical interview.

3.1.9 Environmental Factors

It is important to assess variables in the client's environment that may be contributing to their social anxiety. For example, clients may have people in their lives (e.g., family members, friends, colleagues, or a boss) who contribute to their anxiety by criticizing their behavior unnecessarily. Other clients may have individuals in their social circles who reinforce avoidance behaviors by encouraging them to avoid situations that trigger discomfort, or by offering to do things for the client so that they do not have to confront feared situations. Finally, clients may have lifestyles that provide few opportunities for social interaction. For example, in the case of a client who has no intimate relationships, no friends, and who works from home in a postpandemic world, it may be necessary to find ways to increase the client's social contacts in order to provide opportunities in which they can practice cognitive behavioral treatment strategies. Environmental factors that contribute to a client's social anxiety, or that may prevent the client from overcoming their social anxiety, are typically assessed during the course of a comprehensive clinical interview.

> In some cases, family members and friends of people with SAD may accommodate the person's symptoms

3.1.10 Cultural Factors

It is important to ask clients about any cultural, racial, ethnic, religious, or other identities that may affect their experience of social anxiety symptoms, avoidance, imagery, and so forth. Are there any religious or cultural considerations in terms of avoidance behaviors? Are certain safety behaviors culturally normative for certain groups? Are feared cognitions and images about offending others, bringing shame to one's family, or embarrassing oneself? For a trans individual, are feared cognitions about not passing as a trans man or trans woman? A sensitive assessment of cultural factors that interact with social anxiety is necessary throughout treatment.

3.1.11 Comorbidity

It is important to assess the degree of comorbidity, the relative severity of each comorbid condition, and whether comorbid problems are likely to interfere with the treatment of SAD (e.g., severe depression or substance dependence may require treatment before social anxiety symptoms can be effectively targeted). A helpful option is the DART (McCabe et al., 2021), a modular, semistructured interview for DSM-5-TR disorders that is available at no charge. Information about how to obtain the DART can be found at https://psychiatry.mcmaster.ca/clinical/academic-divisions/anxiety/#tab-content-dart. The DART has demonstrated reliability and validity (Schneider et al., 2022).

3.1.12 Functional Impairment

Assessing impairment in functioning is important for several reasons. First the degree of functional impairment associated with particular aspects of an individual's SAD may influence the target behaviors selected for treatment.

For example, a person who fears public speaking, but who experiences no distress or impairment associated with this fear because they have no interest or need to speak in front of groups, will likely not require treatment for this particular fear. However, the same individual may require treatment for their fear of dating if their inability to speak comfortably with others is impairing and if being in a relationship is one of their goals for therapy.

A second reason for carefully assessing functional impairment is to determine whether interference with functioning is so severe that it needs to be targeted directly during the treatment. For example, if a client's social anxiety has prevented them from ever being in a relationship or holding a job, they may require additional treatment focused on these areas, including vocational counseling and therapy that provides them with the necessary skills to facilitate the development of new relationships.

A number of brief questionnaires are available for measuring functional impairment. One example is the Illness Intrusiveness Ratings Scale (Devins et al., 1983), which assesses impairment in 13 different life domains (e.g., work, social relationships, recreation, financial situation, health). Research with the Illness Intrusiveness Ratings Scale has found impairment in SAD to be significant across most life domains, but particularly high with respect to functioning in social relationships and self-expression and improvement (Antony et al., 1998). Another option is the Ryerson Social Anxiety Scales (Rogojanski et al., 2019) that includes items that measure functional impairment and other severity markers in the context of social anxiety.

3.2   Overview of Effective Treatment Strategies

There are many effective strategies used in treatment protocols to treat SAD. In this section, we have chosen to highlight core strategies that can be clustered into (1) cognitive strategies, (2) exposure-based strategies, and (3) social-skills training. Each of these is described in Table 1.

There is no consistent evidence that combining CBT and medication leads to better outcomes than either approach alone

In addition to psychosocial approaches for treating SAD, there is considerable evidence supporting pharmacological treatments for anxiety disorders, including a variety of antidepressants, anxiolytics, and other medications (Caldiroli et al., 2023; Mayo-Wilson et al., 2014). Medications with support from at least one randomized controlled trial are listed in Table 2. Note that relapse rates tend to be higher following discontinuation of pharmacotherapy than following discontinuation of CBT (Liebowitz et al., 1999). Evidence generally suggests no significant advantage for combining medications and therapy as compared to each treatment on its own (Mayo-Wilson et al., 2014).

Table 1
Evidence-Based Psychological Strategies for Treating Social Anxiety Disorder

Treatment strategy	Description
Cognitive strategies	• Involves learning to identify anxiety-provoking thoughts (e.g., "I will make a fool of myself during a presentation"), and to challenge such thoughts to achieve more realistic, balanced, and flexible thoughts and predictions, after examining the evidence • Clients carry out behavioral experiments to test out the validity of their anxiety-related thoughts and predictions • Video feedback is used to develop a more realistic impression of how they appear to others • Clients revisit painful imagery from past events and update the event's outcome or their ability to cope with the event
Exposure therapy	• Involves confronting anxiety-provoking situations directly until they no longer trigger fear and anxiety • Exposure practices include confronting feared social situations in real life, as well as engaging in simulated exposures or roleplays • Clients reduce and then eliminate safety behaviors when in challenging situations • For clients who fear physical sensations of anxiety, interoceptive exposure (i.e., symptom exposure) may be used (e.g., exercising to become sweaty before entering a social situation)
Social-skills training	• Involves learning to improve social and communication skills through a process of education, rehearsal, and feedback • Behaviors that may be addressed through social-skills training include eye contact, body language, strategies for making small talk, presentation skills, assertiveness skills, teaching skills, strategies for managing conflict, listening skills, and others • Social-skills training is often conducted in the context of behavioral rehearsal, both in real social situations and through roleplay practices

Table 2
Evidence-Based Pharmacological Treatments for Social Anxiety Disorder

Medication	Initial daily dose (and maximum daily dose)	Comments
Citalopram (Celexa)	20 mg (40–60 mg)	SSRI antidepressant
Escitalopram (Cipralex; Lexapro)	20 mg (40–60 mg)	SSRI antidepressant
Fluoxetine (Prozac)	20 mg (80 mg)	SSRI antidepressant. Evidence regarding the use of fluoxetine for SAD is mixed
Fluvoxamine (Luvox)	50 mg (300 mg)	SSRI antidepressant
Paroxetine (Paxil)	20 mg (60 mg)	SSRI antidepressant
Sertraline (Zoloft)	50 mg (200 mg)	SSRI antidepressant
Phenelzine (Nardil)	15 mg (90 mg)	MAOI antidepressant. Rarely prescribed due to side effects, interactions, and dietary restrictions
Venlafaxine XR (Effexor XR)	37.5–75 mg (225 mg)	SNRI antidepressant
Clonazepam (Klonapin; Rivotril)	0.25 mg (4 mg)	Benzodiazepine anxiolytic. May be difficult to discontinue
Alprazolam (Xanax)	0.25 mg (1.5–3.0 mg)	Benzodiazepine anxiolytic. May be difficult to discontinue
Pregabalin (Lyrica)	450–600 mg	Anticonvulsant
Gabapentin (Neurontin)	900 mg (3,600 mg)	Anticonvulsant

Note. Each medication listed is supported by at least one randomized controlled clinical trial. For each medication, generic names are indicated first, with brand names in parentheses. Initial and maximum recommended dosages are those recommended by Health Canada (see Katzman et al., 2014). SSRI = selective serotonin reuptake inhibitor; MAOI = monoamine oxidase inhibitor; SNRI = serotonin norepinephrine reuptake inhibitor.

3.3 Factors That Influence Treatment Decisions

3.3.1 Age and Gender

CBT has been found to be useful for children, adolescents, and adults of all ages. When treating younger children, strategies may need to be adapted to be age appropriate. CBT appears to be equally effective for those who identify as men or women with SAD. Further research is needed on the effectiveness of CBT for individuals with diverse gender identities.

3.3.2 Education

CBT is appropriate for individuals from a wide range of educational backgrounds. For clients with lower levels of education or difficulties with reading or writing, some strategies may need to be adapted. Specifically, language may need to be simplified, written work may need to be limited or eliminated, and imagery-based visual aids can be used to explain core concepts.

3.3.3 Neurodevelopmental Considerations

CBT can be adapted for individuals with high-functioning autism spectrum disorder and other neurodevelopmental considerations (e.g., Bemmer et al., 2021; Riches et al, 2023). Consensus is that an individualized approach be taken so that treatment components can be modified to best meet the needs of each person. For example, social-skills training may be incorporated along with cognitive and behavioral strategies.

> **CBT for SAD is helpful for individuals who have a comorbid autism spectrum disorder and SAD**

3.3.4 Family and Relationship Factors

Generally, people with SAD can be treated effectively without involving family members or significant others. However, it may be useful to include family members in treatment in cases where they are contributing to the individual's anxiety, either by being overly critical of the client or by reinforcing the client's avoidance behavior. For example, if the client's significant other also has social anxiety, they may feel threatened as the client begins to improve and may put subtle pressure on the client not to confront their fears. In such cases, addressing these concerns in one or more treatment sessions that include both the client and the significant other may be useful.

3.3.5 Virtual Therapy

In a postpandemic world, virtual therapies have proliferated. A common form of virtual therapy is group or individual sessions offered by teleconference

CBT for SAD offered in a virtual or teleconference format appears to be similarly effective to CBT offered in person

where all components of in-person therapy are essentially replicated in a virtual environment. Initial evidence suggests that virtual group CBT for SAD has similar outcomes to in-person therapy (Milosevic et al., 2022) and that core techniques such as video feedback can be effectively delivered online as compared to face-to-face (Wild et al., 2023). Virtual therapy offers some practical benefits, such as reduced travel time to sessions, the ability for clients to join sessions from a variety of locations (e.g., on a break at work), and increased access for people in remote areas. On the other hand, virtual therapy for SAD may unintentionally reinforce avoidance for some clients who are having trouble leaving their comfort zones. All factors should be considered when there is a choice for individuals between in-person and virtual therapy options. For creative ideas in offering virtual or remote CBT for SAD, see Warnock-Parkes et al. (2020).

3.3.6 Client Preferences and Expectations

It is generally well established that client preferences and expectations for treatment can influence outcome (e.g., Price & Anderson, 2012). Therefore, it is useful to take client preferences into account when developing a treatment plan. For example, clients who have a strong preference for one approach over another (e.g., medication versus CBT versus combined treatment; individual treatment versus group treatment; virtual versus in-person) should have their preferences honored where possible after hearing about the advantages and disadvantages of each approach, except in such cases in which doing so might be detrimental to the client in some way.

3.3.7 Treatment History

History of previous treatments should be taken into account when making treatment recommendations. If a previous treatment was ineffective, it is important to find out why the treatment did not work initially (e.g., lack of compliance by the client, poorly administered treatment by the therapist), so that possible obstacles can be anticipated and dealt with before they occur. If a previous treatment was effective, it is useful to find out from the client which strategies in particular were useful and to build on those in the current therapy.

3.3.8 Ability to Articulate Cognitions

If a client is unable to articulate the thoughts, beliefs, and predictions that contribute to their anxiety and fear despite extensive attempts by the therapist to identify these cognitions, the client may still respond to behavioral strategies such as exposure and safety-behavior reduction. For clients who cannot use the cognitive strategies effectively, behavioral strategies should be emphasized in treatment.

3.3.9 Anxiety Sensitivity and Fear of Sensations

For clients who are anxious about experiencing physical sensations (particularly sensations that might be noticed by others, such as blushing, sweating, and shaking), strategies for targeting fear of sensations should be included in the treatment. These may include cognitive strategies such as challenging beliefs about physical sensations and conducting behavioral experiments to test out the validity of these beliefs. For example, clients who fear shaking in front of others might be encouraged to purposely allow their hands to shake while filling out a form or a check and test out their predictions about potential negative outcomes.

3.3.10 Severity of Avoidance and Safety Behaviors

The more severe the client's avoidance and safety behaviors, the more important it is to include experiments both about dropping safety behaviors and exposure as significant components of the treatment. In cases where clients avoid very little despite their anxiety, a greater emphasis on cognitive strategies and behavioral experiments may be warranted.

3.3.11 Social Skills

In most cases, people with SAD respond well to treatment even when formal social-skills training is not included as a component of therapy. In fact, social skills may improve on their own as clients reduce safety behaviors, work on challenging their anxiety-provoking thoughts, and begin to experience a reduction in anxiety. Nevertheless, including formal social-skills training, provided in the context of exposure to feared situations, should be included in cases of more severe social-skills deficits, and in cases where social-skills impairment appears to interfere with the client's ability to benefit from other cognitive and behavioral approaches and where dropping safety behaviors has not fully remitted social-skills deficits.

3.3.12 Comorbidity

In cases where a client has multiple problems, it is useful to determine which of these is the principal problem. The principal disorder is typically the one that causes the most functional impairment and psychological distress, and the one for which the client wants treatment. In cases where the comorbid problem is more severe than the social anxiety, it is often best to focus on treating the other condition first. On the other hand, treatment of SAD is appropriate when the social anxiety is the principal problem. Though it is possible to work on more than one problem at a time, it is important that the treatment be focused on a manageable number of issues so that progress can be made.

It is also important to assess the degree to which comorbid problems are likely to have an impact on treatment of SAD. For example, if a client's substance use problems make it difficult to attend regular treatment sessions and follow through on homework assignments without self-medicating, it may be important to treat the substance use disorder first or concurrently with the social anxiety. Similarly, if the client is acutely suicidal or has depression that is so severe they can barely get out of bed, it is important for the client to achieve some stability in their mood before the SAD is tackled. Nevertheless, mild to moderate levels of comorbidity often do not interfere with treatment of SAD and should not exclude an individual from obtaining such treatment.

3.3.13 Group Versus Individual Treatment

> Group and individual therapies are both effective options for many people with SAD

Research supports the use of either group or individual treatment for SAD, with some studies suggesting they are equally effective, and others suggesting better outcomes following individual treatment (Bieling et al., 2022). Factors that should influence the decision of whether to offer group or individual treatment for SAD include availability of group versus individual treatment, the client's willingness to participate in a group, the likelihood of a client being able to participate in a group treatment without compromising the experience for other members of the group (e.g., individuals with significant personality psychopathology might not be a good fit in a SAD group), the extent to which a client appears to be a better fit for individual treatment than group treatment (e.g., perhaps due to comorbid problems, scheduling difficulties, severity of the problem), and the extent to which having others available during treatment sessions (e.g., for exposure role-plays) is important for a particular client.

4

Treatment

Treatments that have been investigated for SAD have included primarily cognitive and behavioral interventions. Therefore, the focus will be on these particular approaches to treatment.

4.1 Methods of CBT

Treatment of SAD typically includes between 10 and 15 weekly sessions, and includes a variety of strategies, such as self-monitoring, psychoeducation, cognitive strategies, and behavioral strategies. For some, a longer course of CBT may be warranted if significant gains have not been made after 15 to 20 sessions (Butler et al., 2021). This section discusses each of these strategies in detail. Methods for preventing relapse and recurrence are also reviewed in this section. Table 3 provides a summary of a sample 12-session protocol for treating SAD using CBT in an individual format. Sessions typically last 50 minutes to an hour. Sessions that include in-session exposure practices and experiments may last longer. Group sessions are typically 90 to 120 minutes. The strategies described in this section have been adapted from protocols by Aderka and Hofmann (2021), Antony and Swinson (2017), Clark and Wells (1995), Heimberg and Becker (2002), Hope et al. (2019), and others. Please note that there are several specific protocols for treating SAD that are not fully incorporated into this section but have evidence to support their use including imagery-based CBT (McEvoy et al., 2018), process-based CBT (Aderka & Hofmann, 2021), and mindfulness and acceptance-based approaches (Kocovski et al., 2013).

Although most studies of CBT for social phobia are based on 10 to 15 sessions, treatment may need to last longer for some

4.1.1 Self-Monitoring

CBT requires that clients monitor their thoughts and behaviors to identify appropriate treatment targets and to measure change over time. The advantage of completing self-monitoring forms or diaries versus simply asking a client to remember their experiences from the previous week is that self-monitoring gets around biases in retrospective recall and limitations in memory. People tend to forget the details of their experience over the course of the week, and their memories are often influenced by how they are feeling at the

Self-monitoring helps clients to take notice of variations in their anxiety symptoms

time they are trying to recall a particular event or experience. For example, if clients are feeling particularly anxious on the day of their therapy session, they may be more likely to recall the entire week as having been more difficult, compared to clients who are feeling less anxious on the day of their therapy session. Other advantages of self-monitoring are that it keeps clients engaged in the treatment process between therapy sessions, it encourages them to notice their symptoms and the variables that affect their symptoms, and it provides them with an opportunity to work through particular treatment strategies and to measure their effectiveness.

Table 3
Session-by-Session Summary of Individual Cognitive Behavioral Therapy for Social Anxiety Disorder (SAD)

Session	Strategies and topics covered
Session 1	• Develop agenda in collaboration with client • Introduction to SAD treatment (e.g., what to expect from treatment, structure and frequency of sessions, importance of homework) • Psychoeducation – model of SAD, overview of treatment strategies, recommended self-help readings • Overview of self-monitoring strategies • Assign new homework – complete monitoring forms, read introductory chapters from self-help readings
Session 2	• Develop agenda in collaboration with client • Review of homework • Psychoeducation – review cognitive model, provide examples of cognitive distortions, and discuss links between client's anxiety and their thoughts • Assign new homework – monitor cognitive distortions, read self-help chapter(s) on cognitive strategies
Session 3	• Develop agenda in collaboration with client • Review of homework • Psychoeducation – review strategies for challenging cognitive distortions • Assign new homework – practice challenging cognitive distortions on thought records
Session 4	• Develop agenda in collaboration with client • Review of homework • In-session behavioral experiment involving using and then dropping safety behaviors in a conversation • Psychoeducation about the role of safety behaviors in maintaining anxiety and detracting from performance and interpersonal connection • Assign new homework – practice experiments of dropping safety behaviors. Record outcomes including anxiety, feelings of connection, and feelings of authenticity. Use thought records to challenge cognitive distortions

Table 3 Continued	
Session	Strategies and topics covered
Session 5	• Develop agenda in collaboration with client • Review of homework • In-session video feedback exercise • Assign new homework – continue experiments of dropping safety behaviors. Record outcomes including anxiety, feelings of connection, and feelings of authenticity. Use thought records to challenge cognitive distortions. Integrate learning from video feedback into thought records
Session 6	• Develop agenda in collaboration with client • Review of homework • Psychoeducation – introduction to exposure • Develop exposure hierarchy • Assign new homework – continue experiments of dropping safety behaviors. Record outcomes including anxiety, feelings of connection, and feelings of authenticity. Use thought records to challenge cognitive distortions. Integrate learning from video feedback into thought records. Work on hierarchy
Session 7 through 10	• Develop agenda in collaboration with client • Review of homework • In-session exposures and role-plays • Incorporate imagery rescripting as needed • Assign new homework – cognitive restructuring, completion of thought records, conduct behavioral experiments, exposure practices
Session 11	• Develop agenda in collaboration with client • Review of homework • In-session exposures and role-plays • Homework – cognitive restructuring, completion of thought records, conduct behavioral experiments, and exposure practices
Session 12	• Develop agenda in collaboration with client • Review of homework • Psychoeducation – discuss triggers for relapse and recurrence, review strategies for preventing relapse and recurrence • Assign new homework – practice relapse prevention strategies

The format of monitoring can be flexible. For some individuals, it may be difficult to complete standard forms, and recording responses in a less-structured diary format may be more useful. For other clients (e.g., children, adults with limited education, clients whose first language is different than the therapist's), monitoring forms may need to be simplified. Some clients may refuse to complete forms altogether, either because they find the process tedious, they are worried about being judged by the therapist for what they record on the forms, or because they find it anxiety provoking to focus on their thoughts, behaviors, and experiences. In these cases, clients should be encouraged to complete at least some self-monitoring despite their reluctance. If their reasons for avoiding self-monitoring are anxiety based, then conceptualizing the filling in of forms as an exposure practice may be useful, and completing forms should become easier over time. The content of written forms can be recorded in other ways, including the use of voice memos on smart phones for clients who prefer this modality.

4.1.2 Psychoeducation

Psychoeducation involves teaching clients about the nature of anxiety, providing them with a framework with which to understand their own social anxiety, helping them to understand the relationships among their anxiety symptoms, anxiety-provoking thoughts, and anxiety-reducing behaviors, and teaching them about effective strategies for dealing with their anxiety. Self-help books (e.g., Antony & Swinson, 2017; Hofmann, 2023) can also be used to reinforce material discussed during treatment sessions.

Presenting the Treatment Rationale

An important focus of the first treatment session in CBT is the presentation of the treatment rationale. It is ideal to engage the client in this discussion, personalizing the content and using questions to elicit the client's perspective whenever possible. Key points to be covered during the first session include the following:

- Anxiety is normal, and everyone experiences anxiety from time to time, in various situations. It is also normal to feel anxious in social situations, and most people report feeling shy, nervous, or anxious at times about the possibility of being judged by others.
- It is useful to recognize that anxiety actually helps us to survive in the world. All of the symptoms that are experienced when one is anxious or frightened help the individual or organism to survive in the face of possible danger or social threat, by preparing the body for escape or for meeting the threat head on, perhaps with an aggressive response. When we are anxious, our hearts race to get blood to larger muscles. We begin to breathe more quickly in order to increase oxygen levels to meet the demands of the situation. We sweat to cool off the body so we can physically perform more efficiently. In addition to these general benefits of anxiety, social anxiety in particular also has advantages. Apprehension about making a bad impression on others helps us to avoid saying things or doing things that might lead to being negatively evaluated or even being ostracized from a group. Anxiety also motivates us to prepare for a social challenge (e.g., a job interview) and to perform the best we possibly can. Social anxiety is only a problem when it occurs so frequently and so intensely that it interferes with an individual's life, such that the costs of the anxiety outweigh the benefits. Therefore, the goal of treatment is not to eliminate all anxiety, but rather to bring anxiety

Clients should be encouraged to think of their anxiety as being normal, and even helpful in certain situations

down to a level where it no longer causes significant impairment. Anxiety consists of three components: the *physical* component (what we feel), the *cognitive* component (what we think), and the *behavioral* component (what we do). The therapist could introduce this by asking the client to reflect on a recent example where they were nervous (e.g., starting therapy) and share how they know when they are anxious. The therapist can then start organizing the client's responses into the three components.

- The physical component of anxiety includes all of the physical sensations that people experience when they are nervous or frightened, including a racing heart, shortness of breath, dizziness, blushing, shaking, and sweating, for example. These symptoms are perfectly normal and completely safe. They occur during anxiety, but they also occur in the context of other intense emotions (e.g., anger), during sexual arousal, during exercise, as well as in other situations.
- The cognitive component of anxiety refers to the thoughts, assumptions, images, beliefs, and predictions that an individual holds about the situations they fear or about their performance (e.g., "It would be terrible to make a mistake during my presentation"), as well as about the symptoms of anxiety themselves (e.g., "People will think I'm disgusting if I sweat at the party"). The cognitive component also includes any biases in attention or memory that influence a person's anxiety. People with SAD often have elevated self-focused attention, focusing on their discomfort and ignoring what is actually happening. People also tend to pay more attention to information that confirms their beliefs and to remember such information as compared to information that is inconsistent with their beliefs. They may also purposely seek out information that confirms their beliefs. For example, during a presentation a socially anxious client may scan the audience for individuals who appear to be bored or to disapprove of their presentation.
- The behavioral component of anxiety refers to behaviors that individuals use to prevent their anxiety from occurring, to reduce the intensity of anxiety after it has begun, or to prevent other negative consequences from occurring. These behaviors may include avoidance, escape, or overreliance on safety behaviors. The physical, cognitive, and behavioral components interact with one another, and the cycle of anxiety can begin with any one of the three components. For example, a sensation of sweating may trigger beliefs about being noticed and negatively evaluated by others, which in turn may trigger an escape from the situation. Similarly, a thought that others will negatively evaluate one's presentation may lead to physical sensations such as shaking and blushing, which in turn can lead to increased anxiety and an avoidance response.
- From a cognitive behavioral perspective, anxiety is not triggered by situations and events alone, but rather by our interpretations and beliefs about these events and what people are afraid of revealing about themselves in that situation (e.g., "People will see that I'm socially awkward"). In particular, anxiety occurs when a situation is perceived as dangerous or threatening. They fear that they will "reveal" negative self-attributes

At the start of treatment, it is important to present clients with a CBT model for understanding their social anxiety

(Moscovitch, 2009). They make negative predictions about what might happen in social situations, they tend to be overly focused on themselves when in social situations, and they dwell on everything that might have gone wrong after a social interaction has ended. In addition, anxiety-related behaviors (e.g., avoidance, escape, safety behaviors) serve to keep the social anxiety alive by preventing individuals from ever learning that feared situations are actually much safer than they seem (e.g., others are often more focused on themselves than the person with social anxiety), feared consequences are unlikely to come true, and that the individual probably can cope with such consequences if they do occur.
- Effective treatment strategies are designed to directly target the three components of anxiety and fear.

4.1.3 Cognitive Strategies

Cognitive restructuring (also called cognitive reappraisal) is closely related to strategies developed by Aaron T. Beck and colleagues (e.g., Beck et al., 1985, see pp. 300–368). The primary goal of cognitive restructuring is to teach clients to identify their anxious thoughts, to consider the evidence regarding these thoughts, and to replace unrealistic or exaggerated beliefs about possible danger with more realistic, balanced, and flexible thoughts, beliefs, and predictions. Clients are encouraged to think of their beliefs as hypotheses, rather than facts, and to consider a range of possible interpretations and outcomes instead of automatically assuming that the worst is likely to happen.

Instead of simply telling clients what they "should" be thinking, cognitive therapy uses Socratic questioning to help clients arrive at their own conclusions based on the evidence. Examples of Socratic questions that can be used to help clients to challenge their anxious thoughts include:
- Are there other ways of thinking about that situation?
- How might someone without social anxiety think about this situation?
- Are your thoughts consistent with the evidence or with previous experiences?
- What else might occur, other than your feared outcome?
- What might you say to a friend who was nervous about having shaky hands at a party? Would you recommend that she never go to another party?
- What if someone noticed you make a mistake? For how long would the person think about you? Would your mistake be the most important thing that has happened in that person's day? What other things might that person be concerned about?
- What if your job interview goes poorly and you do not get the job? How could you cope with that? Does the possibility of that happening mean that you should never apply for a job?
- What if _____ actually finds you boring? Why would that be a problem? What would it mean about you? Are there are other ways of thinking about that?
- Can you think of advantages of staying at the party despite your anxiety?

Table 4 describes a variety of cognitive strategies that can be used to challenge anxiety-provoking thoughts and predictions in people with SAD.

Table 4
Examples of Cognitive Strategies for Social Anxiety Disorder

Strategy	Description
Cognitive restructuring	• Involves asking Socratic questions designed to help the client to recognize that (1) feared outcomes may be unlikely to occur, and (2) they would be able to cope with many of their feared outcomes if they actually were to occur • Also involves completion of thought records on which clients record their anxiety-provoking thoughts, alternative thoughts, and the evidence for and against both the anxious thoughts and the alternative thoughts. The goal of using the thought records is to reduce anxiety by learning to think about feared situations in less anxious ways
Behavioral experiment	• Involves designing and executing experiments to test out whether a particular thought is true • Often used to compare outcomes with and without safety behaviors • Example: doing something to draw attention to oneself (e.g., spilling a glass of water, dropping keys, yelling to someone across a crowded room) to assess whether the belief "it would be terrible to do anything to draw attention to myself" is in fact true
Perspective shifting	• Involves asking a client to take the perspective of someone who is not anxious and to think about the situations that make them anxious from the alternative perspective • Examples: (1) ask the client how their friend (who is not anxious in social situations) might think about a particular anxiety-provoking situation, (2) ask the client what they might say to someone else who reported a thought or prediction similar to that of the client, (3) ask the client to participate in a role-play simulation in which they play the role of the therapist and the therapist plays the role of the client
Survey	• Involves gathering data from objective third parties about the client's anxious prediction/assumption to broaden their perspective • Examples: asking people if they expect all conversations to be "perfect," what they would think of someone who was flushed or sweaty, if they can remember every person who has made a mistake in their presence
Coping statements	• Involves having the client record realistic statements (perhaps derived through earlier cognitive restructuring) that can be used as quick reminders when feeling anxious • Examples of coping statements might include: (1) it is okay if not everyone likes me, (2) it is normal to sweat, shake, or blush in front of others from time to time, (3) I don't have to be perfect

Thought Records

Figure 2 provides an example of a social anxiety thought record that can be used to help people with SAD challenge their anxiety-provoking thoughts whenever they feel anxious about a social situation (a blank copy is reprinted in Appendix 2). In the first column, the client records the date and time when the situation arose and, in the second column, the client provides a brief description of the situation. In the third column, any anxiety-provoking thoughts and predictions are recorded, followed in column 4 by a rating of how anxious the client was (on a scale from 0 to 100). In the next three columns, the client records alternative (nonanxious) beliefs and predictions, evidence and rational conclusions regarding this situation, and their anxiety level after going through the exercise of challenging anxious thinking (again, using a scale ranging from 0 to 100).

Although treatment of SAD includes a number of different strategies, the therapist should take advantage of opportunities to challenge anxiety-provoking thinking whenever possible, including during the homework review at the start of each session. Similarly, clients should be encouraged to challenge their anxiety-provoking predictions during and after exposure practices to challenge postevent rumination that maintains social anxiety symptoms, as evidence suggests that challenging postevent processing can be helpful (Gavric et al., 2023).

A novel CBT protocol for SAD developed by Peter McEvoy and colleagues focuses strongly on anxiety-provoking images in addition to anxiety-provoking thoughts. Thus, the content of some thought records is about challenging negative imagery about what might happen in a social situation. See McEvoy et al. (2018) for more details.

Surveys

Therapists can help the client gather data to come up with a more balanced and realistic perspective using surveys. This can be especially useful when the client engages in mind reading and is having trouble disengaging from an anxious perspective. For example, a client may believe that people can tell they are anxious if they are sweaty and may therefore refuse to go into public places like coffee shops or corner stores. A survey could ask what people think about someone who is sweating in public and how much they notice or care about this. The therapist could set up the survey with open-ended responses or could brainstorm with the client a number of possibilities and see which ones get endorsed. The key with surveys involves establishing the specific information that will be helpful to the client and ensuring that there are enough responses to ensure that responses are not biased in a way that the client can easily dismiss them. Options could include having the therapist send the survey to colleagues (with the client's permission and no identifying information) to gather a broad range of responses. If it is appropriate for the client to share the survey with their friends or family, make sure that they do not send it to others with social anxiety, which could reinforce anxiety-related thoughts!

Day and time	Situation	Anxiety-provoking thoughts and predictions	Anxiety before (0–100)	Alternative thoughts and predictions	Evidence and realistic conclusions	Anxiety after (0–100)
July 12 9 p.m.	I am sweaty at a party.	• People will notice I'm sweaty. • If they notice me sweating, they'll think I'm anxious and weak. • It would be terrible to have others think that I am anxious and weak. • I need to leave this situation before someone notices my sweating.	90	• People may not even notice that I'm sweating. • If they do notice, they may think I am hot or that I am not feeling well. • Even if some people think I am anxious and weak, it wouldn't be the end of the world. • I can stay in this situation despite my anxiety.	• Nobody has mentioned that they notice my sweating, not even my wife. • I notice a couple of other people who seem a bit hot or sweaty. I also notice that some people at the party seem less comfortable than others. • People sweat for all sorts of reasons. I don't think other people are anxious and weak just because they are sweating. • It is impossible for everyone to think positively about me all the time. It is okay if some people think I am anxious or weak. • If I stay in the situation, chances are that my anxiety will decrease. It usually does.	50

Figure 2
Social Anxiety Thought Record. © 2007 Martin M. Antony. Reprinted with permission. A blank version is available in Appendix 2.

Demonstrations

There are a number of videos that can be used as demonstrations of cognitive concepts. For example, this YouTube video helps people learn about attentional biases (e.g., if we are looking for something we find it; if we are not looking for something, we miss it): https://www.youtube.com/watch?v=Ahg6qcgoay4. Another YouTube video helps demonstrate that people do not notice others as much as one might predict: https://www.youtube.com/watch?v=FWSxSQsspiQ.

Behavioral Experiments

A powerful way to challenge anxiety-related predictions is through behavioral experiments. In experiments, the therapist and client collaborate to test out fearful predictions in real time. See Table 5 for examples of behavioral experiments.

Table 5
Examples of Behavioral Experiments in Social Anxiety Disorder

Anxiety-provoking prediction	Experiment	Outcomes to monitor
I will sound stupid if I don't plan what to say.	Have two conversations with a safe person (e.g., colleague of therapist, close friend who knows that the client is in therapy). Plan everything you will say in the first conversation. Focus on what the other person is saying in the second conversation.	Client: How anxious, authentic, and interested were you? Other: How stupid did the client sound in both? Which conversation did you prefer?
I have to stay "invisible" in public to avoid everyone staring and judging.	Do something loud/obvious in public on purpose. For example, drop a handful of change in a busy area, laugh extra loud at a joke or something you are watching on your phone, or wear a garish hat.	How many people stared versus glanced versus did not notice you? How long did people look? Were all reactions negative?
I have to be perfect for others to like me or to succeed.	Hand in a small work or school assignment with a small mistake. Say something "wrong" on purpose in a conversation (e.g., mispronounce a word, get a small fact wrong).	Compare comments and marks with previous assignments that were "perfect." Does the other person end the conversation immediately? Other: Do you prefer to talk to someone who is engaged but imperfect or someone who is perfect?
People won't like me if they see the "real" me.	Have two interactions with someone. In the first, pretend to be someone you think others would like. In the second, be yourself and purposely share an interest or experience.	Client: How anxious, authentic, and engaged were you? Other: How likeable, authentic, and engaged was the client?

The steps to set up a behavioral experiment include the following:
- Identify an anxiety-provoking prediction (e.g., "The cashier at the grocery store will be angry if I need to put an item back").
- Set up the experiment (e.g., purposely pick up an item that you do not need and giving it back to the cashier during checkout).
- Agree on how to evaluate the outcome (e.g., how to know if the cashier is angry – do they raise their voice at the client, roll their eyes, etc.). Please note – therapists need to guide their clients to gather objective data and not make conclusions based on how they feel. Sometimes getting full data about the other's reaction is hard, so the anxiety-related prediction that could also be tested is whether the client can tolerate not fully knowing if the cashier is angry.
- Decide if the therapist will accompany the client on the experiment to help gather data as an observer.
- Conduct the experiment and evaluate the outcome and any conclusions that can be drawn regarding the original prediction.

David Clark's cognitive therapy protocol for SAD (2001) involves early behavioral experiments involving safety behaviors and self-focused attention to help clients realize the negative impacts of these processes and learn valuable information about anxiety-related predictions. For example, the therapist might ask the client to engage in two conversations, the first involving self-focused attention (i.e., monitoring what they are saying and how they are feeling) and safety behaviors (i.e., rehearsing what to say next), and the second with externally focused attention and no safety behaviors. In debriefing this experiment, the therapist should guide the client to consider how anxious they felt in each condition, but also how authentic they felt and how engaged in the conversation they were. Research suggests that eliminating safety behaviors helps clients feel less anxious, more engaged, and more authentic (Dabas et al., 2023).

Consider behavioral experiments early in therapy to gather data about self-focused attention and safety behaviors

Video Feedback

Video feedback is used to help clients gain information about unhelpful and distorted images or perceptions of how they appear in social situations. Clients are asked to engage in a social interaction or performance task on video. Prior to reviewing the video, the therapist guides them to visualize how they think they appeared and make very specific predictions. For example, if the person thinks they will blush, the therapist can use a color chart of shades of pink and red to have the client select the exact shade they imagine themselves having (Warnock-Parkes et al., 2017). If the client thinks they will stammer, the therapist asks the client what they think stammering looks like for them (e.g., missing words, being hard to understand). These feared negative outcomes are rated by the client on a 0- to 100-point scale indicating how much they think the feared outcome occurred. After these very specific predictions are secured, the therapist and client view the video together. It is helpful to have the client view the video in an impartial way, as if they are watching someone else. Their job is to gather objective observational data to

Biased self-images can be challenged effectively using video feedback

Table 6
Samir's Predicted and Actual Fears in Video Feedback Exercise

How I Think I Appear	Prediction	Actual
Long pauses (5+ seconds)	90	30
Hands flapping	100	40
Mouth twitching	70	10

evaluate next to their predictions. Typically, the therapist and client watch the entire video and then reflect on the original predictions of how the client appeared in comparison to what they observed. Sometimes it can be helpful to rewind the video and focus on key moments for the client to see if their predictions were fully supported by evidence. This postvideo review is very important; research suggests that it enhances outcomes as compared to just having the client review the video (Orr & Moscovitch, 2010).

Table 6 gives an example of initial predictions and actual observations from Samir, a university student with significant anxiety about giving a presentation in class. Samir had managed to select classes in his first two years of university that did not involve presentations but was unable to avoid this in his third year. Samir was at risk of failing a current course if he did not do a presentation at the end of semester, so this became a target in therapy. He and his therapist agreed to use video feedback of a mock presentation during a therapy session. Samir shared that his main fears were about looking stupid, losing his place as he talked, and leaving uncomfortable pauses. The therapist used a standard video camera placed on a shelf in the office (although phone cameras can also be used for filming, with the client's consent). After giving the presentation, the therapist engaged Samir in a discussion of Samir's worries about how he would appear.

Therapist: Can you close your eyes and pull up an image of how you think you appeared during your presentation?
Samir: I look stupid ... really awkward.
Therapist: What, specifically, are you imagining that makes you look stupid and awkward?
Samir: Well, I don't know what to do with my hands so they just flap around. And my mouth twitches when I'm nervous.
Therapist: Ok, let's write those down and rate how much you think that happened. Any other predictions about how you appeared or what happened?
Samir: It felt like I took really long pauses as I was going from point to point.
Therapist: How long do you think the pauses were?
Samir: It felt like forever, but maybe 5 seconds? Just really awkward like I don't know what I'm talking about.
Therapist: Ok, let's write that thought down as well.

After Samir recalled and rated his impressions of the presentation, the therapist and Samir reviewed the video together. Samir struggled at first to watch the video objectively, making comments about how "cringey" he looked. The therapist coached Samir to watch from a detached perspective, with a particular focus on the feared images and predictions. After a minute, Samir settled into this stance and was able to watch more objectively. At the end of the video, the therapist asked Samir about the specific predictions. Samir acknowledged that his hands did not flap around like he imagined and the pauses were not as dramatic as they felt. To solidify this point, the therapist suggested they watch a segment of the video again and actually time the pauses. Samir was surprised to discover that the pauses were generally under 2 seconds. The therapist encouraged Samir to keep this information nearby and review it periodically as he prepared for their class presentation.

Sometimes video feedback involves an interaction between the client and someone else (e.g., small talk with someone from the therapist's work setting). In this situation, care should be taken to set up the video (to capture both the client but also the other participant to gauge their reaction and how they appear) and to consider asking the other participant for objective feedback after the interaction to share with the client.

Difficult Memories and Core Beliefs

Clients with SAD often have difficult memories from past social experiences that arise as images and feed into more deeply held beliefs about oneself ("I'm useless") or others ("People are cruel"). Examples could be images of cowering when being verbally bullied by a classmate, standing paralyzed in front of a group while trying to give a presentation, or being teased by peers for mispronouncing a word. These images and beliefs color how they see themselves and many of the situations that arise in their day-to-day lives, feeding into symptoms of social anxiety.

> Core beliefs are deeply held beliefs that affect how an individual interprets most situations that they encounter

A technique for working with negative autobiographical memories and related beliefs is imagery rescripting. After identifying a troubling autobiographical memory, the therapist and client use cognitive restructuring to challenge the negative beliefs related to the memory and then engage in a three-step process. The first step involves the client accessing and reviewing the memory in its original form from the perspective of however old they were when it happened. The second step involves accessing it again from the perspective of their current age. Often these difficult memories occurred in childhood or adolescence so viewing from an adult perspective allows the client to feel compassion for their younger self or realize that the onus for the situation resides more with the bully, peer, other adult, and so forth. The final stage involves reviewing the memory from the perspective of how old they were when it happened, but bringing in their current self to offer support, compassion, or interjection. For example, in the final phase, the client might imagine their adult self assertively standing up to a bully or hugging their child self. See Wild and Clark (2011) for more information on how to use imagery rescripting in SAD. Research suggests that imagery rescripting is helpful for updating images, memories, and beliefs in SAD (Lloyd & Marczak,

> Upsetting social memories can be updated using imagery rescripting, bringing a present, compassionate focus to the memory

2022). Recent work suggests that future-oriented imagery rescripting, where the client rescripts negative imagery about an upcoming social event, can increase willingness to try a behavioral experiment (Landkroon et al., 2022).

4.1.4 Exposure-Based Strategies

Exposure Therapy

> Repeated exposure to feared situations usually leads to a reduction in fear and anxiety

A powerful method of reducing fear is by directly confronting the situations, thoughts, and sensations through exposure therapy. Although there are a number of explanations for how exposure works (see Moscovitch et al., 2009), from a cognitive behavioral perspective exposure is believed to reduce fear and anxiety by providing a corrective experience that contradicts a client's anxiety-provoking thoughts and predictions. Essentially, the client learns that their feared consequences rarely occur (e.g., the client does not make a fool of themselves), and even when bad things happen (e.g., people make a mistake and get laughed at), the situation is more manageable than the client had expected.

Generating Exposure Practices

One of the challenges in using exposure therapy is the generation of appropriate exposure practices. Table 7 includes examples of exposure practices that target fear in particular types of social situations.

Table 7
Examples of Exposure Practices for Social Anxiety Disorder

Feared situation	Examples of exposure practices
Public speaking	• Attend Toastmasters meetings (see www.toastmaster.org). • Take a public speaking course or drama class. • Offer to give a lecture at a high school or elementary school about one's work. • Speak up in meetings at work (e.g., ask questions or volunteer to present some relevant material). • Give a toast at a dinner party. • Ask questions in class. • Read in front of a group.
Small talk and casual conversation	• Arrive at work early and chat with coworkers. • Take advantage of opportunities to attend parties, outings, and get-togethers with friends, coworkers, and acquaintances. • Talk to strangers in public places, such as elevators, lines, and other places. For example, ask what time it is, ask for directions, compliment the other person, or talk about the weather. • Practice joining other conversations that are ongoing (e.g., at a party or gathering). • Attend a gallery opening, a public meeting, or some other gathering of strangers.

Table 7 Continued	
Feared situation	**Examples of exposure practices**
Being observed in public	- Walk down a busy street. - Cross the street at a busy intersection. - Shop in a busy mall or supermarket. - Work out in a crowded gym. - Attend a concert or sporting event. - Sit in a park or coffee shop.
Being the center of attention	- Make a mistake in public (e.g., spill a glass of water, drop keys, purposely lose train of thought, knock something over). - Play a party game (e.g., Pictionary, Outburst, charades). - Tell an anecdote at an online meeting. - Call out to another person from across a crowded room. - Compliment someone on an online meeting. - Arrive late to a meeting. - Wear clothing that is likely to attract comments (e.g., bright colors, mismatched clothes, incorrectly buttoned shirts).
Dating and meeting new people	- Meet others with common interests through meetup.com. - Talk to others who might be possible targets for friendship or dating. - Join an online dating service, answer personal ads. - Join a club or take a class where you might meet people with similar interests (e.g., a fitness club, hockey team, book club, photography class). - Ask a coworker or acquaintance out for lunch, a coffee, drink, or movie. - Offer to drive an acquaintance home from a party or from work.
Eating or drinking in front of others	- Go out for lunch, dinner, or drinks with friends or colleagues. - Eat in a crowded restaurant or food court. - Eat messy foods in front of others. - Purposely allow hands to shake while holding a drink. - Eat or drink in front of others at work or school.
Writing in front of others	- Fill out a check in front of others. - Fill out a form (e.g., a credit card application, a contest ballot) in front of others. - Write a letter while sitting in a public place (e.g., a coffee shop). - Sign documents in front of colleagues. - Purposely allow hands to shake while writing in front of others.
Potential conflict situations	- Drive slowly on a busy street (but be careful not to endanger yourself or other drivers). - Do multiple transactions at a bank machine when the line is long. - Return an item to a store. - Take a long time to make a decision when ordering dinner in a restaurant. - Have a cashier ring up some items in a store and then explain that you have left your wallet at home.

Exposure Hierarchies

> An exposure hierarchy is a list of feared situations arranged in order of difficulty to guide exposure practices

A useful tool in exposure therapy is the exposure hierarchy. An exposure hierarchy is a list of situations that an individual fears and avoids, rank ordered from situations that produce mild anxiety at the bottom of the list, to situations that produce extreme anxiety at the top of the list. For each item, clients provide a fear rating (e.g., using a scale ranging from 0 to 100), and the order of items is determined by these ratings. Typically, exposure hierarchies include 10 to 15 items. Items should generally reflect situations in which the client would like to feel more comfortable, that are practical and easy to arrange during the course of treatment. For example, "getting married" would not be an appropriate hierarchy item for client who is not currently in a relationship. Items on the hierarchy should also be as specific as possible. For example, "going to a party with my wife at the home of a coworker, without drinking any alcohol" would be a more useful item than "going to a party." Table 8 presents an example of an exposure hierarchy for SAD.

Hierarchies are often used to guide exposure practices. Clients begin exposures with items in the bottom half of their hierarchy and, as situations become easier, they progress to more difficult situations. It is not necessary to start with items right at the bottom of the hierarchy. In fact, clients can start as high as they are willing to go. It is also not necessary to practice items in order. In fact, newer perspectives in exposure-based therapies for anxiety disorders suggests that engaging in items in random order may help with new learning and generalizing this learning (see Craske et al., 2014). Items can also be added and deleted as the client progresses through treatment and it

Table 8
Example of an Exposure Hierarchy for Social Anxiety Disorder

Number	Item description	Fear rating (0–100)
1	Share something personal with coworkers	100
2	Start a conversation with a new person	90
3	Ask strangers for directions to a store not in the mall	85
4	Have lunch in the lunchroom with coworkers	85
5	Share my opinion on a current event with co-workers	80
6	Ask a question to multiple coworkers	70
7	Discuss my weekend with coworkers on Monday morning	65
8	Ask strangers for directions at the mall	50
9	Make comments to strangers about the weather on an elevator	50
10	Walk down a busy street alone with my hat on backwards	40

becomes apparent that changes to the hierarchy are warranted. The hierarchy can also be used as a measure of change by having the client rerate the items at each session, or less often (e.g., every third or fourth session).

Guidelines for Effective Exposure

Not all exposure is helpful. In fact, exposure can lead to an increase in fear or anxiety depending on the way it is done. For example, being rejected after spending months working up the courage to ask somebody out on a date can be devastating for somebody with SAD. To get the most out of exposure, it is important for clients to follow a few key guidelines. Research evidence concerning these guidelines is reviewed in more detail elsewhere (e.g., Moscovitch et al., 2009). An exposure and experiment monitoring form is also provided in Appendix 3.

Frequency of Exposure Practices

Exposure seems to work best when practices are scheduled close together. Generally, we recommend that clients engage in major exposure practices (e.g., eating out with colleagues) at least three to four times per week, and small exposure practices (e.g., saying hello to strangers on the elevator) whenever opportunities arise. If exposures are too infrequent, return of fear will be significant, and each practice will seem like starting over. However, if exposures are frequent, they tend to build on one another, and each practice tends to be easier than the one before.

Length of Exposure Practices

Longer exposures tend to work better than shorter exposures. Generally, exposures should last long enough to learn that one's feared consequences do not come true, or to learn that it is possible to cope in a situation despite high levels of anxiety. Often, an individual's anxiety will decrease over the course of an exposure practice. However, evidence suggests that it is not necessary to experience a reduction in fear and anxiety during any particular practice in order to experience improvement across practice sessions (Craske & Mystkowski, 2006). The length of an exposure practice generally depends on the type of situation. For example, a client who is working on decreasing anxiety at parties may choose to stay at a party for several hours, perhaps arriving at the beginning of a party and staying at least until people start to leave. On the other hand, an individual who is afraid of asking for directions might stand in a mall or some other public place and practice asking people for directions repeatedly, for 30 to 60 minutes. The key is to follow a plan and stay until the person has gathered useful data about what happens and their ability to cope. Typically, this will coincide with a decrease in fear. Generally, the longer an exposure lasts and the more it is repeated, the more beneficial it is.

Perceived Control and Predictability

As reviewed by Antony and Swinson (2000), there is evidence that fear reduction during exposure practices is related to a client's perception of control in a situation, as well as the extent to which events seem predictable during the practice. Perceived control can be enhanced by helping clients to recognize that they are more socially skilled than they assume, they are in charge of choosing exposure practices, and they do have some control over what happens to them in social situations.

Eliminating Safety Behaviors

Clients should be encouraged to begin to let go of their safety behaviors. Often this process begins after completing experiments where individuals drop safety behaviors and notice that their feared predictions are unlikely (see Section 4.1.3). This process can occur gradually and can be built into the hierarchy.

Focus on the Task Rather Than the Outcome

Although one goal of CBT is for clients to learn that the outcomes they fear are unlikely, another goal is to learn that these outcomes do occur from time to time, and that they are often more manageable than previously assumed. The initial goal of exposure practices should not be to get a date, land a job, or win over an audience. Of course, as the individual becomes more comfortable, drops safety behaviors, and lets themselves immerse themselves in the experience, they will start to enjoy more positive consequences as well. Following successful treatment, clients will be more willing to risk the possibility of rejection and will be better able to cope when they are evaluated negatively by others. Clients should think a successful exposure is one in which they confront a feared situation despite their anxiety, regardless of the outcome. They should expect to feel uncomfortable and should resist the temptation to fight their anxiety or to try to "make" it go away.

> Exposure is most effective when practices are predictable, prolonged, frequent with no safety behaviors

Social Mishap Exposures

To help clients learn that they can cope with embarrassment, rejection, and other feared outcomes, it may be helpful to encourage clients to engage in social mishap exposures, where they purposely face their worst social fears (Fang et al., 2013). For example, a client might purposely call someone by the wrong name, ask for directions to the store they are standing in front of, or wear mismatched socks or shoes. Often the outcome of even the most feared blunders is not as awful as the client imagined, helping them learn that their feared predictions are more catastrophic than reality.

Symptom Induction

Symptom induction can be used for individuals who are frightened of experiencing particular sensations in social situations. For example, people who are afraid of sweating in front of others might be encouraged to wear warm clothing in social situations to learn that it is okay to sweat in front of other people. They might even wet their foreheads or underarms before going into social situations to learn that nothing bad actually happens when one appears sweaty. People who are frightened of blushing in front of others might do things to make their faces red, such as eating spicy foods, eating hot soup, wearing blush, holding their breath, or exercising. People who

> Exposure to feared sensations, such as sweating, may be useful for people who fear these symptoms

fear shaking in front of others might be encouraged to purposely shake their hands as they speak in front of a group, hold a drink, fill out a form, or sign their names. Specific exercises have been developed for inducing a wide range of sensations that people often experience when feeling anxious (see Antony, Ledley, et al., 2006). Generally, people with SAD are not frightened of physical sensations when they are not in the company of others. Therefore, when treating SAD, symptom exposure should be combined with situational exposure practices.

Troubleshooting

A number of issues can interfere with a client's progress during exposure therapy. Table 9 provides a list of possible obstacles, along with strategies for overcoming these challenges.

Table 9
Exposure Therapy Obstacles and Possible Solutions

Obstacle	Possible solutions
Fear does not decrease during an exposure practice	• Increase the length of the practice. • Assess whether the client is relying on safety behaviors during the practice and, if so, attempt to eliminate these behaviors. • Assess the degree to which a client's anxious thoughts and predictions are contributing to the lack of fear reduction, and address these using cognitive strategies. • Note that fear reduction during a particular exposure practice is not necessary for long-term benefit from exposure therapy. If fear does not decrease despite attempting some of the solutions already discussed, resume exposure practices at the next session.
Fear returns between exposure practices	• It is normal for some degree of fear to return between exposure practices. If return of fear is significant, assess whether life events or circumstances (e.g., a critical boss, an abusive partner) are contributing to the return of fear. Also, consider scheduling exposure practices more frequently.
Client refuses to do a particular practice	• Negotiate with the client to come up with a new practice that is challenging but manageable. • Ask the client whether the proposed practice can be altered in some way to make it more manageable.
Client requests to end the practice due to fear	• Encourage the client to continue the practice by providing reassurance that their fear will decrease over time. • Use cognitive strategies to bring the fear down to a manageable level. • Alter aspects of the situation to bring the fear down to a manageable level. • If the client ends up terminating the exposure practice, encourage them to enter the situation again as soon as possible.
Client is not fearful of the practice	• Exposure requires fear activation to be effective. If a client is not fearful of a particular practice, alter aspects of the situation to make the practice more challenging, or attempt a different practice from the client's hierarchy.

Table 9 Continued	
Obstacle	Possible solutions
The situation is too brief for prolonged exposure	• Exposure practices are most effective when they are prolonged. In the case of a brief exposure (e.g., asking for directions, paying for items in a store, standing in line), it is best to repeat the practice over and over, until the client's anxiety has decreased or the client has learned that their fear consequences do not occur.
Social skills impairments interfere with exposure outcomes	• Clients with significant social-skills impairment may find that their feared consequences actually occur on a regular basis (e.g., a client who avoids all eye contact may find that others show no interest in talking to them). In these cases, it may be important to work on social-skills impairments during exposure practices (e.g., encouraging the client to make more eye contact when talking to others).

4.1.5 Social-Skills Training

Social-skills training is based on the assumption that social anxiety is, in part, related to impairments in social skills, which in turn lead to negative reactions from others, thereby confirming the individual's view of themselves as inadequate. Social-skills training involves identifying behaviors to target, educating clients about appropriate social behavior, encouraging clients to practice new social behaviors, and providing feedback to the client about their use of these strategies. Social skills are typically rehearsed in the context of simulated role-play exposures as well as real-life exposure practices. Often, practices are video recorded so clients can view their performance. Video recording is useful because it provides clients with an opportunity to more objectively judge the quality of their performance, relative to making such judgments without actual data. Video recording also provides the therapist with opportunities to provide clients visual examples of behaviors that need to be worked on. Examples of social skills that are often targeted during social-skills training are provided in Table 10. A number of excellent self-help guides are available for improving social and communication skills (e.g., McKay et al., 2018; Paterson, 2022).

4.2 Mechanisms of Action

Theories regarding the mechanisms underlying the effectiveness of cognitive behavioral treatments for SAD have ranged from cognitive explanations to behavioral theories and models involving emotional processing.

Table 10
Examples of Social Skills Targeted in Social-Skills Training

Social skill	Examples of behavioral goals
Nonverbal communication	• Improving frequency of eye contact • Learning to lean forward when sitting with others • Standing closer to others • Smiling more frequently (or less frequently in clients with a tendency to smile or laugh when nervous) • Sitting up straight
Speech patterns	• Learning to speak with a confident tone • Increasing the volume of speech (for clients who speak too quietly) • Speaking with more expressiveness in one's tone
Conversation skills	• Using conversation starters – strategies for breaking the ice • Being able to generate ideas for small talk • Learning strategies for ending conversations gracefully • Apologizing less frequently (for clients who tend to apologize constantly – even when they have not done anything that requires an apology)
Listening skills	• Maintaining eye contact when listening to others • Conveying understanding and empathy when listing to others • Avoiding barriers to effective listening, including comparing oneself to the other individual, rehearsing what to say next, changing the subject, filtering what the other person says, etc.
Assertiveness skills	• Stating one's needs without being perceived as pushy or aggressive • Using the "broken record" technique – repeat one's needs without excessively justifying or explaining one's perspective • Confronting issues directly with other people, rather than passively • Learning to listen assertively, with a commitment to understand the other person's perspective • Learning to validate the other person's feelings
Conflict skills	• Choosing appropriate times to discuss sensitive issues • Staying focused on the problem at hand • Using cognitive strategies to examine whether one's perspective is realistic • Deciding whether a confrontation is worth the potential consequences • Trying to understand the other individual's perspective • Bouncing ideas off a neutral third party before discussing the issue with the other individual
Interview skills	• Preparing for interviews (e.g., learning about the organization, preparing a list of questions, identifying one's strengths) • Listening to what the interviewer asks and says • Dressing appropriately for the interview • Knowing how to answer personal questions • Learning to appear confident, flexible, courteous, and tactful • Managing the postinterview phase appropriately (e.g., following up with the interviewer)
Dating skills	• Developing strategies for meeting new people (e.g., networking, personal ads, joining clubs, or taking classes) • Improving conversation skills • Managing issues that arise during different stages of dating (e.g., the first meeting versus knowing the person for several months) • Dealing with rejection

Table 10 Continued	
Social skill	Examples of behavioral goals
Presentation skills	• Preparing for the presentation (e.g., understanding the purpose of the presentation, understanding the audience, preparing slides or other materials, rehearsing, using CBT strategies to manage anxiety) • Make sure that all words are pronounced correctly, that voice volume does not drop off, that rate of speech is appropriate, and that words such as "um" and "uh" are avoided • Increasing expressiveness in one's tone • Making eye contact with audience members • Walking around the presentation, and gesturing with one's hands • Resisting the temptation to read the presentation verbatim • Repeating the main points frequently • Resisting the temptation to fit in too much information • Avoiding the tendency to talk down to the audience, while being sure to explain new concepts fully • Being prepared to answer questions • Being genuine (i.e., not trying too hard to be entertaining) • Using humor where appropriate

4.2.1 Cognitive Models

Cognitive models of SAD suggest that CBT works by helping clients accumulate evidence to disconfirm negative predictions. Exposure-based strategies can also be understood from a cognitive perspective (Antony et al., 2020; Moscovitch et al., 2009). Exposure therapy provides clients with new experiences that challenge previous beliefs that feared situations are dangerous, which in turn lead them to spend more time in these situations, thereby further disconfirming their anxious predictions.

Some research suggests that change in cognition fuels change in symptoms. For example, reductions in maladaptive beliefs about one's self predicted later reductions in social anxiety symptoms across group CBT (Gregory et al., 2018), as did increased self-efficacy about challenging negative cognitions in individual CBT for SAD (Goldin et al., 2012). Reductions in overestimations of negative outcomes also appears to explain symptom change in SAD (Calamaras et al., 2015; Gregory et al., 2015).

4.2.2 Behavioral Models

A number of behavioral theories have been used to explain the effects of CBT and, particularly, the effects of exposure-based treatments, as well as social-skills training. These include constructs such as habituation, extinction, and reinforcement-based approaches.

Habituation is frequently mentioned in the CBT literature as a possible mechanism underlying the effects of exposure. Habituation is a natural, universal perceptual process that leads to a reduced response to a stimulus over time. It is also associated with a reinstatement of the response after a break from the stimulus. For example, when first entering a room with fresh-cut flowers, a person would likely be very aware of the smell of the flowers, but gradually would get used to the flowers and stop being aware of the smell. However, after leaving the room and returning, the individual's awareness of the smell of the flowers returns. As reviewed by Moscovitch et al. (2009), the notion of habituation does not adequately explain the effects of exposure, in part because individuals do not always experience reduction in fear during exposure, and because complete reinstatement of fear in between sessions often does not occur. In fact, most clients experience a reduction in fear across sessions. Finally, habituation is an automatic perceptual process, rather than one involving new learning. Yet it is well established that fear reduction following exposure does involve new learning (Moscovitch et al., 2009).

An alternate behavioral explanation for the effects of exposure involves extinction learning. According to Pavlovian conditioning theory, extinction is defined as a decrease in responding that occurs when a conditioned stimulus is presented repeatedly in the absence of an unconditioned stimulus (e.g., when an individual repeatedly engages in public speaking and discovers that there are no negative consequences). Extinction does not involve unlearning of a previously learned association; rather, it is believed to be an active learning process in which people come to associate safety with a previously feared situation (Rescorla, 2001). As reviewed by Moscovitch et al. (2009), an extinction model appears to fit the data regarding the effects of exposure better than a habituation model. Furthermore, an extinction model is not necessarily incompatible with a cognitive understanding of the mechanisms underlying exposure. It is widely believed that cognitive factors such as information processing are involved in extinction learning.

Building upon an extinction model is the notion of inhibitory learning. Inhibitory learning suggests that new safety learning inhibits original fear associations such that fear associations are not extinguished, but rather inhibited. This model suggests that CBT provides the individual various pieces of safety learning through cognitive and behavioral strategies. This model also suggests that the return of fear is possible if the person stops gathering safety learning to inhibit fear associations, placing a strong emphasis on ongoing relapse prevention work for individuals. See Craske et al. (2014), Tolin (2019), and Weisman and Rodebaugh (2018) for a more detailed account.

Finally, some behavioral models assume that problem behaviors are a function of environmental contingencies. In other words, they persist over time because they are reinforced by the individual's environment. For example, avoidance of feared social situations persists over time because of negative reinforcement associated with the relief that the individual experiences when they escape from the feared situation. By deciding to stay in a feared situation, rather than escaping, the individual prevents the sudden and powerful experience of relief, thereby breaking the cycle of avoidance and the associated negative reinforcement.

4.2.3 Emotional Processing Models

> According to emotional processing theory, the client's fear needs to be activated during exposure practices to work

Emotional processing theories are based on the assumption that fear is represented as a networked memory structure containing three types of information: (1) information about a feared object or situation (e.g., a party), (2) information about one's responses to the feared stimulus (e.g., avoidance, sweating), and (3) information about the meaning of the feared stimulus and fear responses (e.g., the assumption that sweating at a party is threatening). In their classic emotional processing model, Foa and Kozak (1986) proposed that altering an emotional memory requires activation of the fear network and encoding of new information that is incompatible with the information originally stored in emotional memory. Exposure-based treatments are believed to be effective because they activate an individual's associative fear network (including stimulus, response, and meaning elements of the fear), and incorporate new, nonthreatening information into the network.

4.3 Efficacy

4.3.1 Efficacy of CBT

> Cognitive and behavioral techniques, in various combinations, are effective for reducing symptoms of SAD

Numerous studies have demonstrated that CBT is an effective treatment for SAD, with sustained effects up to 12 months posttreatment (van Dis et al., 2020). Typically, treatments include various combinations of cognitive and behavioral strategies. They may be delivered in a group or individual format, and generally both approaches seem to be effective (Mayo-Wilson et al., 2014).

Comparing CBT Components and Formats
Exposure Versus Cognitive Therapy Versus Combination
Five major meta-analyses have attempted to answer the question of which treatment components are most effective for treating SAD (Chambless & Hope, 1996; Federoff & Taylor, 2001; Feske & Chambless, 1995; Gould et al., 1997; Taylor, 1996). Across meta-analyses, all of these strategies have been found to have moderate to large effect sizes in comparison to wait-list control conditions. However, these meta-analytic studies differ with respect to the question of whether cognitive restructuring plus exposure is more effective than exposure alone. For example, Gould et al. (1997) found that exposure had the largest effect sizes of all the strategies (either when administered alone or with cognitive restructuring). Feske and Chambless (1995) found no differences between exposure alone and exposure combined with cognitive restructuring. Finally, Taylor (1996) found that only treatments combining cognitive restructuring and exposure were more effective than placebo. Effect sizes for cognitive restructuring alone, exposure alone, and social-skills training alone were equivalent to those for placebo.

Studies focused specifically on the Clark and Wells (1995) and Clark (2001) protocol have found that cognitive therapy with behavioral experiments is helpful as compared to exposure (Clark et al., 2006) and interpersonal psychotherapy (Stangier et al., 2011), in group format (Colhoun et al., 2021), and offered via the internet with therapist support (Clark et al., 2023).

Social-Skills Training
Although there is little evidence from controlled studies to support the use of social-skills training alone as a treatment for SAD, studies suggest that social-skills training may lead to enhanced outcomes when added to other CBT strategies (e.g., cognitive restructuring and exposure), compared to these strategies without social-skills training (e.g., Beidel et al., 2014).

Individual Versus Group Treatment
Research on the relative effectiveness of group versus individual treatment for SAD has been equivocal. Several meta-analyses have failed to find differences in the effectiveness of individual versus group therapies (Barkowski et al., 2016; Federoff & Taylor, 2001; Gould et al., 1997; Taylor, 1996). However, one recent network meta-analysis found both treatments effective, with individual CBT demonstrating the largest changes across treatment (Mayo-Wilson et al., 2014).

Technology-Assisted CBT
Studies have investigated several ways that CBT for SAD can be offered with the assistance of technology. One example is internet-based CBT (iCBT) for SAD where CBT strategies are offered via online materials, most often with some limited therapist support to help the client personalize and apply the strategies. A meta-analysis of iCBT supports the efficacy of iCBT with therapist support for SAD at posttreatment, as well as 6- and 12-month follow-up (Guo et al., 2021), finding that iCBT yielded similar outcomes to traditional CBT. Similarly, a recent study by Clark and colleagues found that iCBT based on Clark's model of SAD required half the therapist hours to achieve the same outcome as traditional CBT on social anxiety symptoms (Clark et al., 2023), though traditional CBT was associated with stronger behavioral outcomes. Another form of technology-assisted CBT for SAD is virtual reality exposure therapy where individuals perform SAD exposures in a virtual environment (e.g., giving a speech to a virtual audience). Studies suggest that virtual reality exposure therapy is similarly effective to in-person exposure for reducing symptoms of social anxiety (Kampmann et al., 2016) and may be associated with lower drop-out rates (Chowdhury & Khandoker, 2023). A text message intervention encouraging the reduction of safety behaviors outperformed a comparison group who received text messages encouraging present focus (Cougle et al., 2020). Various forms of technology-assisted CBT will no doubt be a focus of ongoing work on ensuring all individuals with SAD receive high quality therapy.

4.3.2 Predictors of Outcome

A number of variables have been studied as possible predictors of treatment outcome in individuals with SAD, including symptom severity, comorbid depression, anger issues, use of safety behaviors, severity of cognitive distortions, interpersonal problems, attachment-style treatment expectancies, and homework compliance. Research suggests many of these variables improve across treatment but do not necessarily predict treatment outcome. Some evidence exists that higher scores of safety behaviors and cognitive distortions predicted better outcomes in individual CBT (Butler et al., 2021). Severity of social anxiety predicts poorer outcomes in some studies (Otto et al., 2000), but not in others (Butler et al., 2021). The effects of comorbid depression on outcome have been mixed. A recent individual-level meta-analysis found that comorbid depression did not negatively affect outcomes, and that higher levels of depression were associated with better outcomes in individual CBT (Rozen & Aderka, 2021). Erwin et al. (2003) found that problems with anger predicted dropout from a 12-session group CBT treatment for SAD, as well as a poorer treatment response among those who completed treatment.

> A client's expectations regarding treatment have been found to predict treatment outcome

Various process variables have been found to impact upon treatment. Two studies (Chambless et al., 1997; Safren et al., 1997) found that clients who expected a more positive outcome from CBT tended to do better during treatment. Similarly, compliance with CBT homework has been found to predict outcome in several studies (e.g., Conklin et al., 2021; Leung & Heimberg, 1996). Increases in group cohesion (i.e., the extent to which group members feel supported by and affiliated with one another) over the course of group CBT have also been found to be related to be more positive outcome in one study (Taube-Schiff et al., 2007), though a previous study using a different measure of group cohesion (Woody & Adessky, 2002) found no relationship between group cohesion and treatment outcome.

4.3.3 Patterns of Change

Some research has investigated how and when people change in CBT for SAD. Sudden gains occur in CBT for SAD (one study found that they occurred in 18% of cases), but do not predict outcome for all individuals with SAD (Kivity et al., 2022). For those who show a rapid response, symptom change appears to be encouraged by changes in fears of negative evaluation (Auyeung et al., 2020). Anxiety levels fluctuate in early exposures and do not predict outcome, but the relationship between anxiety during exposure and subsequent treatment outcomes grows stronger as therapy progresses (Hayes et al., 2008).

4.3.4 Preventing Relapse and Return of Symptoms

Little has been written on predictors of relapse in the treatment of SAD. However, based on their clinical experience, Ledley and Heimberg (2005) suggest two variables that may contribute to relapse and recurrence of symptoms. The first is continued avoidance of social situations, and the second is a failure to generalize the treatment strategies and practices to new situations.

Preparation for termination should begin at the first treatment session. Clients should be informed that treatment is unlikely to remove all of their social anxiety symptoms. Rather, the goal of treatment is to teach the client to be their own therapist, so that they can continue to work on the social anxiety even after treatment has ended. The exercises used during treatment should focus on helping the client to manage anxiety in the context of feared situations that arise in their daily life, and the client should be encouraged to apply the treatment strategies to new situations that arise after the end of treatment.

There are a number of specific methods that can be used to reduce the likelihood of relapse after successful treatment (Ledley & Heimberg, 2005). First, clients should have reasonable and realistic expectations regarding their functioning after treatment has terminated. Although most clients improve during treatment for SAD, many continue to struggle with occasional anxiety, and may still avoid some situations. Clients should be taught that it is normal to feel anxious in social situations from time to time. Efforts should be made to instill confidence in the client's ability to continue using the treatment strategies once treatment has ended. In particular, it may be useful for clients to continue monitoring safety-behavior use, plan experiments when needed, and to take advantage of exposure opportunities when they arise. Periodically, clients should take stock of where they are in their lives with respect to their social anxiety, and to examine their short-term, medium-term, and long-term goals. Regularly scheduled booster sessions, in person, on video, or over the telephone, may also be useful to keep clients on track after treatment has ended. In addition, encouraging clients to become involved in valued activities that involve regular social contact is likely to be useful. For example, clients may attend regular meetings of Toastmasters, join a volleyball league, or become more active in their communities. Occasionally rereading relevant self-help books or joining a local anxiety support group may also be useful.

4.4 Combination Treatments

Pharmacotherapy is an effective treatment for SAD, either alone or in combination with CBT. This section reviews the use of medication treatments for SAD, followed by a review of studies examining the relative and combined effects of pharmacotherapy and CBT (i.e., cognitive strategies and/or behavioral strategies) for this condition.

4.4.1 Medication Treatments

SSRI antidepressants and venlafaxine are the medication treatments of choice for SAD

Table 2 (Chapter 3) provides a list of evidence-based medication treatments for SAD, including recommended initial and maximum dosages. A wide range of antidepressants has been found to be effective for treating SAD, including selective serotonin reuptake inhibitors (SSRIs), monoamine oxidase inhibitors, and serotonin norepinephrine reuptake inhibitors (Katzman et al., 2014). The most well-studied medications are the SSRIs and the serotonin norepinephrine reuptake inhibitors, while some medications like moclobemide have only been studied in small trials (Caldiroli et al., 2023; Mayo-Wilson et al., 2014). Certain benzodiazepines, such as clonazepam and alprazolam have been found to be useful for treating SAD, and there is also evidence supporting the use of gabapentin and pregabalin, which are both anticonvulsants. There are a number of medications with emerging evidence for the treatment of SAD that are being studied off label (for a review, see Caldiroli et al., 2023).

A detailed review of the evidence supporting these and other medications is available in the Canadian Psychiatric Association's "Canadian Clinical Practice Guidelines for the Management of Anxiety, Posttraumatic Stress and Obsessive-Compulsive Disorders" (Katzman et al., 2014).

Medications approved by the US Food and Drug Administration for the treatment of SAD include paroxetine, paroxetine controlled release, sertraline, and venlafaxine. Despite its effectiveness, phenelzine is rarely used to treat this disorder because of potentially severe side effects, frequent interactions with other medications, and strict dietary restrictions (foods containing tyramine, including certain cured meats, cheeses, and wines, for example, must be avoided). SSRIs and venlafaxine are typically considered to be first-line treatments for this condition and are usually well tolerated by clients. Commonly reported side effects include gastrointestinal symptoms, sleep disturbance, and headache, and these often improve over time. In some clients, symptoms of agitation, tremor, and anxiety may occur early in treatment, and also tend to improve over time. These symptoms can be managed by starting at lower dosages and increasing dosages gradually. Weight gain and sexual side effects are also common, and these symptoms often continue over the course of treatment. Most SSRIs and venlafaxine are usually easy to discontinue, though paroxetine discontinuation is often associated with "flu-like" withdrawal symptoms due to its short half-life. Therefore, it is important to discontinue paroxetine more gradually than might be the case for other SSRIs.

Benzodiazepines may be an option for individuals who have difficulty tolerating antidepressants, who need a bridge to start other medications, as well as for individuals taking medication as needed. Though antidepressants typically take several weeks to have an effect, the therapeutic effects of benzodiazepines are usually experienced within an hour or less. The most common side effects of benzodiazepines include sedation, physical changes (e.g., changes in balance), and cognitive impairment (e.g., memory impairments). There are also potential effects on babies for mothers who use benzodiazepines while pregnant. Because of concerns about possible dependency, benzodiazepines should usually be restricted to short-term use, and should be used with great caution in older adults and individuals with a history of substance abuse. Discontinuation of benzodiazepines should be completed at a gradual pace to minimize withdrawal symptoms. Further, benzodiazepine use may become a safety behavior; clients in CBT may find it helpful to have a discussion about this with their therapist. See Edinoff et al. (2021) for a thorough discussion of the risks and benefits of benzodiazepine use.

4.4.2 Comparing and Combining Medications and CBT

Although there are differences among individual studies with respect to the effectiveness of combining CBT and various medication treatments, summarizing across studies suggests that pharmacotherapy, CBT, and their combination are about equally effective for the treatment of SAD, particularly in the short term (Mayo-Wilson et al., 2014). Follow-up findings suggest that psychological treatments are less susceptible to relapse and recurrence relative to medication treatments, though more long-term studies are needed.

Medication and CBT tend to work about equally well, with little evidence of enhanced outcomes by combining them

Augmentation of Exposure with D-Cycloserine

D-cycloserine is an agonist of the glutamatergic N-methyl-d-aspartate receptor that traditionally has been used to treat tuberculosis and has also been found to facilitate extinction learning in animals. There has been strong interest in d-cycloserine as a possible enhancer of the effects of exposure therapy for phobias. Evidence across multiple studies suggests that d-cycloserine taken before or after exposure sessions for SAD leads to better outcomes on a number of variables than placebo plus exposure therapy (Guastella et al., 2008; Hofmann et al., 2006; Smits et al., 2020). However, unlike other medications used to treat social anxiety, d-cycloserine is not an anxiolytic. On its own, this drug has little to no effect on anxiety. Rather, d-cycloserine is believed to work by enhancing learning and therefore it has been studied only in the context of exposure-based treatments.

Studies suggest that d-cycloserine combined with exposure therapy may lead to better outcomes than exposure alone

4.5 Overcoming Barriers to Treatment

4.5.1 Treatment Ambivalence

Clients often have mixed feelings about receiving CBT. Research on people with anxiety disorders including SAD used the Treatment Ambivalence Questionnaire (Rowa et al., 2014) and found that concerns clustered into three areas: (1) fears of the personal consequences of engaging in treatment (e.g., "This treatment will change my personality"), (2) fears of negative or adverse reactions to treatment (e.g., "I won't get better"), and (3) concerns about the inconvenience of treatment (e.g., "Treatment will be time consuming"). Asking clients with SAD about their treatment concerns can be a fruitful opening to discussing ambivalence.

There are a number of approaches to dealing with ambivalence about treatment. One strategy is to identify cognitive and behavioral factors that contribute to ambivalence, and to target these using CBT strategies. For example, a client who is convinced that treatment will fail might be encouraged to examine the evidence for and against this belief.

Perhaps the best-known method for dealing with treatment ambivalence is *motivational interviewing* (Miller & Rollnick, 2023). Motivational interviewing involves ways of talking with clients about change to understand and hopefully strengthen motivation and commitment to change(Miller & Rollnick, 2023). Some of the key assumptions of motivational interviewing include the following:

- People are ambivalent about change. For example, although a client may recognize that avoidance of social situations limits opportunities, they may also be aware that avoidance prevents the rejection that sometimes occurs when social risks are taken.
- To benefit from treatment, the client must be *willing*, *able*, and *ready* to change. In other words, the client must believe that change is an important priority, and that they will be able to change, once provided with the right tools.
- The focus of motivational interviewing is on intrinsic reasons for change (e.g., changes that are consistent with the client's personal values), rather than on extrinsic reasons (e.g., financial gains, social pressure).

In motivational interviewing, the therapist is encouraged to reduce behaviors that are likely to increase client resistance. These include arguing for change, assuming an expert role, accepting diagnostic labels as an explanation of the client's behavior, and being in a hurry for the client to change. Instead, the therapist highlights and amplifies the discrepancy between the client's values and goals on the one hand, and their current behavior on the other hand. The therapist expresses empathy, supports the client's efforts to develop self-efficacy, and encourages the client to generate intrinsic reasons for change. The therapist "rolls with resistance," rather than targeting resistance directly or advocating for change, which are believed to amplify resistance.

> Motivational enhancement strategies may be useful for clients who are ambivalent about treatment

Research investigating motivational interviewing prior to CBT for SAD has produced equivocal results. Westra and Dozois (2006) studied 55 participants with SAD, panic disorder, or GAD. Individuals received either three sessions of motivational interviewing or no pretreatment sessions prior to receiving group CBT. Motivational interviewing was associated with a stronger response to treatment, as well as greater compliance with homework. On the other hand, Peters et al. (2019) found that motivational interviewing prior to CBT for SAD did not generally improve treatment outcomes, though it appeared to be helpful for people with high functional impairment but not for those who had high readiness to change. Three sessions of motivational interviewing also did not appear to improve ambivalence for those with SAD (Romano & Peters, 2021). These studies all offered motivational interviewing as a separate pretreatment intervention; it is possible that motivational interviewing strategies interspersed within other CBT strategies when needed might produce better outcomes for ambivalent clients (see Aviram et al., 2016).

4.5.2 Homework Noncompliance

Several studies have found homework compliance to be correlated with a more positive outcome following CBT. Homework helps to reinforce the strategies learned during therapy sessions and facilitates the generalization of skills to naturalistic settings and situations that often cannot be targeted within the treatment session.

Improving homework compliance depends on first being able to identify the reasons why a client is not completing homework. Possible reasons for homework noncompliance may include (1) not understanding the task, (2) homework assignments are not relevant to the client, (3) homework tasks are too frightening, (4) interpersonal issues, (5) other demands on the client's time, and (6) failure of the therapist to ask about homework at the beginning of each session.

Once the reasons for homework noncompliance have been identified, attempts can be made to improve compliance by targeting the specific issue. For instance, if a client's noncompliance is related to homework complexity, it may be useful to simplify homework assignments or simplify forms, for example. Providing homework instructions in writing may also be helpful, and illustrating homework practices in session first will ensure that the client understands what is expected when they attempt the practice for homework.

In the case of exposure homework, noncompliance is often due to fear. Even in cases in which the client was able to enter a situation during a therapy session, repeating the practice for homework, without the therapist present, may be difficult. If a practice is too difficult, the therapist should encourage less frightening homework practices. Scheduling telephone contacts between sessions may also be helpful. Clients often leave a therapy session feeling confident about being able to complete homework; however, over the next few days, confidence may fade. A short phone call may help to boost the client's confidence to the point that homework can be completed.

If lack of compliance appears to be related to poor organization, scheduling conflicts, or demands on the client's time, a problem-solving approach may be useful for improving homework completion. Key steps include identifying barriers to homework completion, brainstorming possible solutions, evaluating each potential solution, selecting the best solution, and, finally, implementing the selected solution. For example, a client who is having difficulty finding time to socialize with others may try combining social activities with other tasks and activities that they are already engaged in (e.g., eating with others instead of eating alone).

In some cases, a lack of homework compliance may indicate poor motivation for treatment. For these clients, motivational enhancement strategies may be useful, as discussed in Section 4.5.1. Finally, arriving at a mutual decision to take a break from therapy may sometimes be appropriate, particularly for clients who are clearly not invested in the treatment.

4.5.3 Adapting Treatment for Comorbidity

Many people with SAD present with a number of different additional problems, including other anxiety disorders, depression, substance use disorders, or other psychological disorders. There is little to no research regarding the best ways to treat SAD in the context of other disorders.

For individuals who have comorbid anxiety disorders, treatment may focus first on the most significant problem, followed by treatment of any additional anxiety disorders later. However, an alternative is to treat the various anxiety disorders concurrently. There is evidence that a unified anxiety disorders treatment can be used effectively for people with a wide range of anxiety disorder diagnoses (see Barlow et al., 2015).

> **CBT for SAD may be a highly effective treatment when substance use is a safety behavior**

For individuals with other types of comorbidity, it is important to assess the relative severity of the individual's SAD and other disorders. If the other conditions are milder and somewhat under control, it may be possible to focus on the SAD without much attention to the other conditions. In cases where the other disorders are severe, and their symptoms are likely to have an impact on the treatment of SAD, it may be necessary to treat the other condition first, or to treat the SAD and other conditions concurrently. Concurrent treatment makes the most sense when the SAD and other conditions appear to be functionally related. For example, a client who drinks excessively because of social anxiety might not respond well to a treatment that focuses exclusively on the social anxiety or on the alcohol use. Rather, an integrated treatment that targets the core features of both problems might be best.

4.6 Adapting Treatment for Different Age Groups

4.6.1 Children and Adolescents

SAD is a common problem in children, with prevalence of symptoms exceeding threshold for likely SAD estimated at 36% across multiple countries (Jefferies & Ungar, 2020). The basic strategies used to treat SAD in children and adolescents are similar to those used in the treatment of adults, with a focus on cognitive restructuring, exposure, and social-skills training. However, when treating younger individuals, strategies are typically adapted to be age appropriate. For example, instead of an exposure hierarchy, the metaphor of an *exposure stepladder* is often used, where each rung of the ladder represents an exposure step. In addition, because it is often difficult for children to appreciate the long-term benefits of conducting exposure practices, rewards are often used to reinforce completion of exposure practices and other treatment-related tasks. These may include stickers, money, toys, or special privileges at home (e.g., staying up late to watch a favorite television show). Another example of how treatment may be adapted for children is the use of a *fear thermometer* instead of the standard 0–100 numerical scale that adults use to rate their levels of fear. Children are asked to indicate their fear level during exposure practices by pointing to the appropriate location on a picture of a thermometer, in which the bottom of the thermometer indicates low levels of fear, and a top of the thermometer indicates high levels of fear.

Cognitive tools may also need to be adapted for children. For example, thought records may need to be simplified, and the rationale for cognitive restructuring must be explained at an age-appropriate level. In very young children, it may be difficult to use cognitive strategies because the child may be unable to identify their anxiety-provoking beliefs.

When treating children, it is common practice to include parents in the treatment. This is important because it is typically the parents who will ensure that treatment homework is completed between sessions. It is also useful for parents to learn strategies to stop any behaviors that may function to reinforce the child's anxiety or avoidance (e.g., allowing the child to stay home from school when feeling anxious). If a parent suffers from social anxiety, it may be helpful for that parent to seek treatment. Modeling nonfearful behavior in front of the anxious child may facilitate the child's recovery.

A number of excellent resources (for therapists and parents) exist on the treatment of anxiety disorders in children in general (e.g., Chorpita, 2007; Rapee et al., 2022), as well as books on treating SAD in particular (Albano & DiBartolo, 2007a, 2007b; Eisen & Engler, 2007; Kearney, 2005; Shannon, 2022).

4.6.2 Older Adults

SAD has been found to have a lifetime prevalence of 6.6% among adults over 60 years of age in the United States (Kessler et al., 2005), and 4.94% for older adults in Canada (Cairney et al., 2007). Although these estimates are lower than those for general adult samples (Kessler et al., 2005), they suggest that SAD continues to be a significant problem as people age. Nevertheless, there are very few studies examining the treatment of anxiety disorders in older adults, and almost all of these have been focused on GAD.

One treatment study to include older adults with SAD (Schuurmans et al., 2006) compared CBT to sertraline (an SSRI) for a mixed sample of older adults with various anxiety disorders, including SAD, GAD, panic disorder, and agoraphobia. Generally, CBT was found to be effective, though the effect sizes for sertraline were stronger. Data on the outcome of treatment for specific anxiety disorders were not presented in this study, so it is impossible to know the effects of treatment on SAD, in particular.

In treating older adults, several factors need to be taken into account (Ayers et al., 2007). First, medical comorbidity can complicate the assessment and treatment of anxiety in this population. Many of the physical symptoms of anxiety can look similar to symptoms of medical illness, so it is particularly important for the individual to have a thorough medical workup. Similarly, memory loss can make it difficult for some individuals to complete CBT assignments. A study by Mohlman et al. (2003) included memory aids and strategies such as between-session telephone calls to increase homework compliance in a study of older adults with GAD. Because this study found larger effect sizes than typical studies of CBT in older adults with GAD, it is possible that such aids can enhance treatment outcome in this population. Finally, it is important to recognize that aging is often associated with interpersonal losses (e.g., death of a spouse, loss of family members and close friends) that may cause social anxiety to suddenly become an important issue for the first time. In such cases, treatment should emphasize helping the client to develop the skills necessary for expanding their social circle.

4.7 Adapting Treatment Across Diverse Groups

SAD appears to occur across cultures, ethnic groups, and diverse populations. Although presentations of SAD have broad similarities across ethnic and cultural groups, there are also culture-specific ways in which SAD may present. Studies suggest that CBT is effective across a number of diverse groups, though more research is needed on cultural adaptations of CBT for SAD. For example, in a review of seven case studies of cultural adaptations of CBT for SAD, Jankowska (2019) concluded that treatment outcomes were generally promising with culturally specific modifications to treatment.

Therapists should become acquainted with the ways in which culture has an impact on symptoms that may otherwise be associated with SAD, including cultural expressions of distress, cultural values that may impede engagement in therapy, level of acculturation, language in which therapy is offered, cultural values on authority, cultural norms about "taboo" topics, and cultural impact on the therapeutic relationship. For example, Yoshinaga et al. (2013) describe cultural adaptations of CBT for a client from Japan where the therapeutic relationship needed to be more directive and formal given cultural norms for how individuals view authority figures. In another case study with a South Korean immigrant, care was taken to understand the importance of cultural values on family and group harmony (Ashworth et al., 2011). Similarly, in CBT for an Arab college student in the United States, attention was paid to *adab*, which refers to the Islamic etiquette of good manners, morals, decorum, decency, and humaneness (McIndoo & Hopko, 2014).

Considerations for language are also important for individuals whose first language may differ from the therapist's. For example, Weiss and colleagues (2011) suggest asking the client in which language they express emotion and in which language they think, as they might express emotion in their native language more fluidly. Although it may be difficult to match clients with therapists who share their first language, some clients may find it easier to express their feared thoughts, beliefs, and predictions in their native language. Therapy can be adjusted so that clients summarize the results of experiments or discussions in therapy in their first language even if the discussion with the therapist is in their shared language. For clients whose proficiency in the shared language with their therapist is lower than their native language, therapy pace can be slowed down to ensure better comprehension, or therapy can include an interpreter.

Views on the therapeutic relationship may differ across cultures and ethnic groups. In many collectivistic cultures, the therapist is seen as an authority figure and thus may need to be more directive and active in therapy. For example, Toyokawa and Nedate (1996) suggest that it may be difficult for therapy to persist as fully collaborative for clients from collectivist cultures, with the therapist needing to assert and lead the therapy more than would be typical in individualistic cultures. In some cultures, it may be important to ask how a client prefers to be addressed so as not to assume that first names are appropriate. In many East Asian cultures, the value of group harmony may lead the client to agree with the therapist, even if they disagree, necessitating consistent check-ins by the therapist about client buy-in, questions, and progress (Weiss et al., 2011).

Another consideration for clients from collectivistic cultures is to be sensitive about exploring topics that could reflect negatively on family or are "culturally taboo" (Jankowska, 2019). For example, exploring difficult historical family events may be less fruitful for clients where the value of family supersedes individual goals. Techniques like imagery rescripting of family-based difficult events may be less helpful for these clients. Instead, focusing on current goals and challenges may be more palatable. It is also important that clients align their therapy goals with their cultural values; encouraging someone from a collectivist culture to practice assertiveness with authority figures may be a gross mismatch of values. McIndoo and Hopko (2014) discuss the importance of cultural restrictions in establishing therapy goals and tasks. For example, for clients from certain cultures or religious backgrounds, it may be more acceptable to have conversations with same-sex partners. These considerations are important discussions to have with clients when constructing exposures or experiments.

When working with clients from marginalized groups, it is essential to consider that they have likely experienced adverse events including racism, prejudice, oppression, and discrimination that affect their social anxiety as well as their level of trust in a therapist from a different background. The minority stress model (Moradi, 2013) overlaps with CBT models of social anxiety in several ways, suggesting that individuals who have experienced discrimination have increased surveillance or vigilance for further negative reactions from others and use impression management to conceal or minimize their marginalized identity. Thus, therapists need to be sensitive when conducting cognitive work or designing experiments and exposures about

CBT for SAD is highly effective for individuals from diverse backgrounds with modest cultural modifications

realistic evidence the client might have of their feared outcomes occurring in addition to anxiety-related concerns. Safety of the client and helping them cope in the face of discrimination are important therapy goals for clients with SAD who may continue to experience discrimination. Therapists should also ask clients about their use of safety behaviors to conceal their identity, and when it might be safe or unsafe to drop these safety behaviors. For example, for someone from the lesbian, gay, bisexual, transgender, queer/questioning, plus (LGBTQ+) community, it may be objectively unsafe to share their sexual orientation in some environments and therefore therapy would focus on dropping this self-concealment behavior only in objectively safe environments. Meidlinger and Hope (2014) share an example where revealing one's identity as a gay man might lead to his family disowning him due to cultural or religious beliefs about sexual orientation, necessitating a careful discussion about the costs, benefits, and risks of disclosing.

5

Case Vignette

This chapter describes a case example of an individual with SAD, along with the treatment plan.

Working With Jin's Generalized Social Fears

Jin was a 21-year-old gay cis-gendered man from a traditional South Korean family. He lived with his parents, older brother, and grandparents. He attended the University for Health Sciences with the goal of applying to medical school. He presented for treatment with a broad range of social evaluative concerns including fears of being the center of attention in any social situation, fears of being judged for being gay, and fears of revealing social incompetence by saying or doing the wrong things when interacting with others, especially authority figures like professors. He had come out to a few close friends within the Korean Canadian community, but not his family or his non-Korean classmates. As a result of his fears, Jin avoided joining clubs and attending social events for the LGBTQ+ population on campus and he kept quiet in his classes. He also engaged in a number of safety behaviors such as overpreparing for his classes in case he was called upon, rehearsing answers to potential questions during class, and saying little in casual conversations with peers. These safety behaviors were taking their toll on Jin; he was exhausted from overpreparing for classes but missed much of the content during class due to being "in his head" and rehearsing answers. His grades were suffering as a result. He also felt disconnected from most classmates and peers outside of his close group of Korean friends.

Jin completed 20 sessions of individual CBT for his SAD. Session 1 included psychoeducation about SAD and CBT as well as learning more about the specific concerns and beliefs that Jin held and his goals for therapy. The therapist asked about these concerns in the context of Jin's traditional Korean family, knowing that South Korea is a collectivist culture with a strong value on family. Indeed, Jin talked about his worry that not doing well in school or doing something embarrassing in social settings would bring shame to his family. The therapist validated these concerns while also questioning whether Jin's strategy of rehearsing answers was helping him achieve his best in class. Jin agreed to try a behavioral experiment the next session (Session 2) where he listened to one of the therapist's colleagues talk about a recent news story with and without rehearsing potential answers to questions the colleague might ask. In the experiment, the colleague asked Jin questions about the news story after they shared the details. Jin rated his level of anxiety, comprehension, and interest in the subject after each condition. While level of anxiety was similar in both conditions, Jin's ratings of comprehension and interest in the subject were significantly higher when he dropped his safety behavior. With Jin's consent, the therapist also asked their colleague for feedback to share with Jin about Jin's comprehension, engagement, and how much the colleague enjoyed talking with Jin. The therapist also asked the colleague to rate how anxious Jin appeared in both conditions. They reviewed this feedback in Session 3. Much to Jin's surprise, the feedback was dramatically more positive in the condition where Jin dropped his safety behavior, including the confederate's perception of Jin's level of anxiety. The therapist used Socratic dialogue to help Jin process these results, with Jin reflecting that perhaps staying engaged in the conversation provided a better impression to others and did not damage his ability to answer potential questions. The therapist also took the opportunity to explore realistic "worst case scenarios" if Jin did not have a perfect answer to a question in class. Jin shared a catastrophic image of him sitting mutely with the professor and his classmates jeering at him and the associated shame that his parents and grandparents would feel. The therapist gently challenged this image with evidence of times where Jin's classmates did not have well-articulated answers where Jin acknowledged that his professors and classmates did not shame the person and the lecture moved on. The therapist asked Jin to adjust the image to be more consistent with this evidence and practice thinking of this image when he worried about his performance in class.

Sessions 4 through 8 continued to focus on Jin's concerns about his performance in class, which was an important goal for Jin and also less anxiety provoking than some of his social anxiety with peers. While the safety-behavior experiment was enlightening for Jin, the overriding cultural emphasis on presenting well to authority figures like his professors meant his anxiety was "sticky" in this area. The therapist respectfully navigated Jin's cultural beliefs when helping Jin set goals for how he would like to interact with his professors. For example, Jin shared that arriving late for class was highly anxiety provoking, both because he felt like the center of attention, but also because he felt this was disrespectful to his professor. To respect this belief, the therapist and Jin explored other exposures that Jin could do in class and at school that helped challenge his anxiety but did not feel disrespectful to Jin. They created an exposure hierarchy for school, including asking questions in class, approaching the professor with a question after lecture, and sitting in seats closer to the front of the lecture hall. Jin practiced these exposures in multiple classes, with multiple professors. Jin noticed that his anxiety began to settle after practicing these exposures on a daily basis at school. However, in Session 7 he reported that his anxiety had peaked again because of one of his exposures not having gone well. He shared that he approached a professor after class with a question about the readings as per his exposure goals, and the professor had been short with him. Jin worried that he had offended the professor in some way, which spiked his anxiety and caused him to ruminate about the interaction for several days afterward. When he arrived for his session, the therapist and Jin took time to explore this difficult outcome.

Therapist: It sounds like your automatic assumption is that you offended your professor when you asked your question. What makes you sure of that?
Jin: She just seemed distracted and irritated. It must have been my question.
Therapist: Are there any other reasons professors might seem that way?
Jin: What do you mean?
Therapist: Well, professors are people too. I'm just curious if there can be other reasons a person appears distracted or irritated. Can we brainstorm that a bit?
Jin: Ok.
Therapist: For example, what else might be going on in your professor's life outside of this class?
Jin: Well, she runs a research lab. She told us about a big grant application that she is working on right now.
Therapist: That's interesting. Do you think grant applications are stressful and distracting?
Jin: I imagine so. They sound like a lot of work.
Therapist: And what about her personal life. Is it possible that she has things going on outside of school?
Jin: I never think about my professors as having personal lives. But yes, she must.
Therapist: Is it possible that she has things in her personal life that can be distracting at times?
Jin: Of course. I just never think about that.
Therapist: So, do we know for sure that her reaction was because of you and your question?
Jin: I guess not. I would just never want to offend her.
Therapist: I wonder if that value you place on your professors sometimes clouds your reaction and makes you take their reactions personally when it might not be because of you.
Jin: That's possible. I didn't consider that at first.

At Session 9, Jin reported feeling more comfortable with interactions in class. He had stopped rehearsing answers in his head and felt much more engaged and less tired after classes. Given this positive momentum, the therapist used part of Session 9 to broach another important area of Jin's social anxiety: his fear of judgment from his non-Korean acquaintances and classmates in casual conversation or if he joined LGBTQ+ clubs or activities on campus. The therapist first talked to Jin about his experiences as a gay man within his friend group, larger community, and family. Jin reported that his family would probably be supportive, but he had not disclosed his sexuality because he did not want to risk bringing shame to them from the larger community. This fear

Table 11
Jin's Exposure Hierarchy

Number	Item description	Fear rating (0–100)
1	Sharing sexual orientation with acquaintances	100
2	Attending an LGBTQ+ event on campus	95
3	Helping plan an LGBTQ+ event on campus	95
4	Wearing a Pride pin	90
5	Talking about upcoming Pride events with acquaintances	80
6	Sharing anime tastes with acquaintances	70
7	Going into the LGBTQ+ association and asking a question	65
8	Sitting near the LGBTQ+ association on campus	60
9	Sharing musical tastes with acquaintances	50
10	Calling the LGBTQ+ association on campus with a question	40

was reinforced by several difficult experiences that Jin shared where he was teased in high school for looking "feminine," and bullies made disparaging remarks about his sexual orientation. Jin was fearful that peers outside of his close friend group would react in this way. The therapist validated Jin's fears and labeled the bullying behavior as such. Keeping this in mind, the therapist also probed Jin about whether it might be personally important to join the LGBTQ+ community on campus and why. Jin shared that not having any gay friends made him feel a little bit isolated and that he wanted to be proud of his identity. The therapist and Jin collaboratively brainstormed some exposure targets (see Table 11 for his exposure hierarchy).

When constructing Jin's hierarchy, the therapist asked Jin about safety behaviors, especially self-concealment behaviors that Jin was using. Jin shared that he was careful to not talk about certain music tastes or his preferred anime for fear that these interests would reveal something about his identity that acquaintances would judge. Instead, Jin tried to keep conversations with acquaintances on topics that felt "neutral" and would not link Jin to the LGBTQ+ community. The therapist helped Jin label these as self-concealment behaviors and to consider the negative side effects they were having on Jin. Jin agreed that concealing his identity in most situations was tiring and felt disingenuous. Thus, deliberate exposures where he revealed parts of his identity through interests and ultimately self-disclosure were added to the hierarchy.

In Sessions 10 through 17, Jin worked through his hierarchy. The first several steps went smoothly. The members of the LBGTQ+ association on campus were helpful and welcoming when he called or went in person. Jin also reported a positive side effect of sharing his musical and anime tastes when he met another classmate with very similar interests. He realized that most people were open to hearing about his tastes even if they did not share them. No one seemed to actively judge him or make discriminatory comments about his interests. However, he encountered a challenge when he began the exposure of wearing a Pride pin. For the first several days of the exposure, Jin was mainly on campus where his peers either did not even comment or notice his pin or made supportive comments like asking where he got the pin so they could wear one too. However, Jin encountered a difficult experience in a store where an employee at a store made a discriminatory comment to a colleague that Jin overheard. Jin immediately left the store and removed his Pride pin. The therapist asked Jin more about this in their next session.

Therapist: I'm so sorry to hear what happened to you. That's unacceptable.
Jin: It just proves to me that I was right. Everyone is against me.
Therapist: Can we challenge that statement? Have you had any recent experiences that disprove that everyone is against you?
Jin: Ok, I know you're referring to people on campus. But they're different. I can't be myself off campus.
Therapist: Would it be helpful to gather more information about what happens off campus if you share parts of your identity? What if that person doesn't represent everyone? But perhaps in a way where you feel safer.
Jin: What do you mean?
Therapist: What if you continued your exposure, but tried it a few times with one of your close friends? That way, you won't be alone if someone says or does something discriminatory.
Jin: But isn't that a safety behavior to bring someone?
Therapist: Well, it could be, but I also want to make sure you're well supported as you try this. You might not need someone in most situations, so you can see how it goes and then we can decide if you're ok to continue on your own.
Jin: Ok, I can do that.

Jin took a close friend who also wore a Pride pin and attended multiple stores and events off campus. He was relieved to find out that the incident of discrimination did not recur over the next few weeks, which allowed him to gain more confidence that he could wear his Pride pin consistently without being regularly harassed. The therapist made sure to talk with Jin about what he could do or say to cope with any future discrimination or harassment in case he encountered that again.

By Session 18, Jin had tried almost everything on his hierarchy. His scores on measure of social anxiety were below clinical cutoffs, and he reported feeling "lighter," more authentic, and much less tired than he had when he started therapy. The therapist and Jin agreed to move toward termination.

They spent the final two sessions talking about how Jin could maintain gains and anticipating situations that might trigger a return of anxiety and how Jin could manage this. The therapist talked about the value of ongoing "safety learning" to inhibit Jin's original fear associations. They looked for opportunities for Jin to continue building new habits that would gather safety data, like joining committees and groups on campus, consistently asking professors questions, and wearing his Pride pin regularly. Jin agreed to keep his therapy notes handy and review them regularly over the upcoming 6 months. The therapist also offered Jin booster sessions that Jin could book on an as-needed basis.

6

Further Reading

Readings for Professionals

DiBartolo, P. M., & Hofmann, S. G. (2026). *Social anxiety: Clinical, developmental, and social perspectives* (4th ed.). Academic Press.
This book is for readers interested in theory and research on the phenomenology and clinical features of social anxiety disorder.

Heimberg, R. G., & Becker, R. E. (2002). *Cognitive-behavioral group therapy for social phobia: Basic mechanisms and clinical strategies*. Guilford Press.
This book is a seminal text on providing group CBT for social anxiety disorder.

Hofmann, S. G., & Otto, M. W. (2017). *Cognitive behavioral therapy for social anxiety disorder: Evidence-based and disorder specific treatment techniques* (2nd ed.). Routledge. https://doi.org/10.4324/9781315617039
This book delves into specific cognitive behavioural therapy techniques for social anxiety disorder.

Hope, D. A., Heimberg, R. G., & Turk, C. L. (2019). *Managing social anxiety: A cognitive behavioral therapy approach* (therapist guide; 3rd ed.). Oxford University Press. https://doi.org/10.1093/med-psych/9780190247591.001.0001
This book provides an evidence-based protocol for treating social anxiety disorder, written as a therapist guid.

McEvoy, P. M., Saulsman, L. M., & Rapee, R. M. (2018). *Imagery-enhanced CBT for social anxiety disorder*. Guilford Press.
This book provides an imagery-enhanced version of CBT for social anxiety disorder for readers interested in focusing more on imagery work in therapy as compared to traditional verbally-focused CBT.

Weeks. J. W. (Ed.). (2014). *Wiley-Blackwell handbook of social anxiety*. Wiley-Blackwell.
This volume reviews social anxiety disorder from an epidemiological, clinical, and theoretical basis. Readers interested in a broad overview of theory and research on SAD will find this useful.

Readings for Consumers

Antony, M. M., & Swinson, R. P. (2017). *The shyness and social anxiety workbook: Proven, step-by-step techniques for overcoming your fear* (3rd ed.). New Harbinger Publications.
This self-help workbook walks readers through a variety of evidence-based strategies for managing social anxiety, including cognitive strategies, behavioral strategies, mindfulness-based approaches, and medications.

Butler, G. (2016). *Overcoming social anxiety and shyness: A self-help guide using cognitive behavioral techniques* (2nd ed.). Little, Brown Book Group.
This self-help book helps the reader understand the development of social anxiety and then offers practical cognitive and behavioral techniques to manage anxiety.

Fleming, J. E., & Kocovski, N. L. (2013). *The mindfulness and acceptance workbook for social anxiety and shyness: Using acceptance and commitment therapy to free yourself from fear and reclaim your life*. New Harbinger Publications.
This book describes how mindfulness and acceptance strategies can help manage social anxiety symptoms.

Hofmann, S. G. (2023). *CBT for social anxiety: Simple skills for overcoming fear and enjoying people*. New Harbinger Publications.
This self-help manual helps readers with a number of strategies to help with social anxiety, including how to conduct "social mishap" exposures to challenge your worst-case scenarios.

Hope, D. A., Heimberg, R. G., & Turk, C. L. (2019). *Managing social anxiety: A cognitive behavioral therapy approach* (workbook; 3rd ed.). Oxford University Press. https://doi.org/10.1093/med-psych/9780190247638.001.0001
This client workbook is the companion to the therapist guide noted above. It contains helpful self-help worksheets and examples of cognitive behavioural skills for social anxiety.

7

References

Aderka, I. M., & Hofmann, S. G. (2021). Social anxiety: A process-based treatment approach. In D. H. Barlow (Ed.), *Clinical handbook of psychological disorders: A step-by-step treatment manual* (6th ed., pp. 108–132). Guilford Press.

Aderka, I. M., Hofmann, S. G., Nickerson, A., Hermesh, H., Gilboa-Schechtman, E., & Marom, S. (2012). Functional impairment in social anxiety disorder. *Journal of Anxiety Disorders, 26*(3), 393–400. https://doi.org/10.1016/j.janxdis.2012.01.003

Agosti, V., Nunes, E., & Levin, F. (2002). Rates of psychiatric comorbidity among U.S. residents with lifetime cannabis dependence. *American Journal of Drug and Alcohol Abuse, 28*(4), 643–652. https://doi.org/10.1081/ada-120015873

Albano, A. M., & DiBartolo, P. M. (2007a). *Cognitive-behavioral therapy for social phobia in adolescents: Stand up, speak out* (therapist guide). Oxford University Press. https://doi.org/10.1093/med:psych/9780195307764.001.0001

Albano, A. M., & DiBartolo, P. M. (2007b). *Cognitive-behavioral therapy for social phobia in adolescents: Stand up, speak out* (workbook). Oxford University Press. https://doi.org/10.1093/med:psych/9780195307764.001.0001

Ambusaidi, A., Al-Huseini, S., Alshaqsi, H., AlGhafri, M., Chan, M., Al-Sibani, N., Al-Adawi, S., & Qoronfleh, M. W. (2022). The prevalence and sociodemographic correlates of social anxiety disorder: A focused national survey. *Chronic Stress, 6*, 1–9. https://doi.org/10.1177/24705470221081215

American Psychiatric Association. (2013). *Diagnostic and statistical manual of mental disorders* (5th ed.).

American Psychiatric Association. (2022). *Diagnostic and statistical manual of mental disorders* (5th ed., text rev.).

Antony, M. M., Coons, M. J., McCabe, R. E., Ashbaugh, A., & Swinson, R. P. (2006). Psychometric properties of the Social Phobia Inventory: Further evaluation. *Behaviour Research and Therapy, 44*(8), 1177–1185. https://doi.org/10.1016/j.brat.2005.08.013

Antony, M. M., Ledley, D. R., Liss, A., & Swinson, R. P. (2006). Responses to symptom induction exercises in panic disorder. *Behaviour Research and Therapy, 44*(1), 85–98. https://doi.org/10.1016/j.brat.2004.12.005

Antony, M. M., Roemer, L., Lenton-Brym, A. P. (2020). Behavior therapy: Traditional approaches. In S. B. Messer & N. J. Kaslow (Eds.), *Essential psychotherapies: Theory and practice* (4th ed., pp. 111–141). Guilford Press.

Antony, M. M., Roth, D., Swinson, R. P., Huta, V., & Devins, G. M. (1998). Illness intrusiveness in individuals with panic disorder, obsessive-compulsive disorder, or social phobia. *Journal of Nervous and Mental Disease, 186*(5), 311–315. https://doi.org/10.1097/00005053-199805000-00008

Antony, M. M., & Swinson, R. P. (2000). *Phobic disorders and panic in adults: A guide to assessment and treatment*. American Psychological Association. https://doi.org/10.1037/10348-000

Antony, M. M., & Swinson, R. P. (2017). *The shyness and social anxiety workbook: Proven, step-by-step techniques for overcoming your fear* (3rd ed.). New Harbinger Publications.

Ashbaugh, A. R., McCabe, R. E., & Antony, M. M. (2020). Social anxiety disorder. In M. M. Antony & D. H. Barlow (Eds.), *Handbook of assessment and treatment planning for psychological disorders* (3rd ed., pp. 180–212). Guilford Press.

Asher, M., & Aderka, I. M. (2018). Gender differences in social anxiety disorder. *Journal of Clinical Psychology, 74*(10), 1730–1741. https://doi.org/10.1002/jclp.22624

Asher, M., Hermesh, H., Gur, S., Marom, S., & Aderka, I. (2019). Do men and women arrive, stay, and respond differently to cognitive behavior group therapy for social anxiety disorder? *Journal of Anxiety Disorders, 64*, 64–17. https://doi.org/10.1016/j.janxdis.2019.03.005

Ashworth, K. J., Randall, J., Millen, A., & Rosqvist, J. (2011). Culturally competent CBT: Treating SAD in a Korean immigrant – A single case analysis. *Clinical Case Studies, 10*(6), 449–465. https://doi.org/10.1177/1534650111435163

Auyeung, K., Hawley, L. L., Grimm, K., McCabe, R., & Rowa, K. (2020). Fear of negative evaluation and rapid response to treatment during cognitive behaviour therapy for social anxiety disorder. *Cognitive Therapy and Research, 44*(3), 526–537. https://doi.org/10.1007/s10608-020-10077-5

Aviram, A., Westra, H. A., Constantino, M. J., & Antony, M. M. (2016). Responsive management of resistance in cognitive-behavioral therapy for generalized anxiety disorder. *Journal of Consulting and Clinical Psychology, 84*(9), 783–794. https://doi.org/10.1037/ccp0000100

Ayers, C. R., Sorrell, J. T., Thorp, S. R., & Wetherell, J. L. (2007). Evidence-based psychological treatments for late-life anxiety. *Psychology and Aging, 22*(1), 8–17. https://doi.org/10.1037/0882-7974.22.1.8

Barkowski, S., Schwartze, D., Strauss, B., Burlingame, G. M., Barth, J., & Rosendahl, J. (2016). Efficacy of group psychotherapy for social anxiety disorder: A meta-analysis of randomized-controlled trials. *Journal of Anxiety Disorders, 39*, 44–64. https://doi.org/10.1016/j.janxdis.2016.02.005

Barlow, D. H., Conklin, L. R., & Bentley, K. H. (2015). Psychological treatments for panic disorders, phobias, and social and generalized anxiety disorders. In P. E. Nathan & J. M. Gorman (Eds.), *A guide to treatments that work* (4th ed., pp. 409–461). Oxford University Press. https://doi.org/10.1093/med:psych/9780199342211.003.0014

Beard, C., Rodriguez, B. F., Moitra, E., Sibrava, N. J., Bjornsson, A., Weisberg, R. B., & Keller, M. B. (2011). Psychometric properties of the Liebowitz Social Anxiety Scale (LSAS) in a longitudinal study of African Americans with anxiety disorders. *Journal of Anxiety Disorders, 25*(5), 722–726. https://doi.org/10.1016/j.janxdis.2011.03.009

Beck, A. T., Emery, G., & Greenberg, R. (1985). *Anxiety disorders and phobias: A cognitive perspective*. Basic Books.

Beesdo-Baum, K., Knappe, S., Fehm, L., Höfler, M., Lieb, R., Hofmann, S. G., & Wittchen, H.-U. (2012). The natural course of social anxiety disorder among adolescents and young adults. *Acta Psychiatrica Scandinavica, 126*(6), 411–425. https://doi.org/10.1111/j.1600-0447.2012.01886.x

Beidel, D. C., Alfano, C. A., Kofler, M. J., Rao, P. A., Scharfstein, L., & Sarver, N. W. (2014). The impact of social skills training for social anxiety disorder: A randomized controlled trial. *Journal of Anxiety Disorders, 28*, 908–918. https://doi.org/10.1016/j.janxdis.2014.09.016

Bemmer, E. R., Boulton, K. A., Thomas, E. E., Larke, B., Lah, S., Hickie, I. B., & Guastella, A. J. (2021). Modified CBT for social anxiety and social functioning in young adults with autism spectrum disorder. *Molecular Autism, 12*(11). https://doi.org/10.1186/s13229-021-00418-w

Bieling, P. J., McCabe, R. E., & Antony, M. M. (2022). *Cognitive behavioral therapy in groups*. Guilford Press.

Blöte, A., & Westenberg, P. M. (2007). Socially anxious adolescents' perception of treatment by classmates. *Behaviour Research and Therapy, 45*(2), 189–198. https://doi.org/10.1016/j.brat.2006.02.002

Bögels, S. M., van Oosten, A., Muris, P., & Smulders, D. (2001). Familial correlates of social anxiety in children and adolescents. *Behaviour Research and Therapy, 39*(3), 273–287. https://doi.org/10.1016/S0005-7967(00)00005-X

Bostwick, W. B., Boyd, C. J., Hughes, T. L., West, B. T., & McCabe, S. E. (2014). Discrimination and mental health among lesbian, gay, and bisexual adults in the

United States. *American Journal of Orthopsychiatry, 84*(1), 35–45. https://doi.org/10.1037/h0098851

Buckner, J. D., Heimberg, R. G., Matthews, R. A., & Silgado, J. (2012). Marijuana-related problems and social anxiety: The role of marijuana behaviors in social situations. *Psychology of Addictive Behaviors, 26*(1), 151–156. https://doi.org/10.1037/a0025822

Butler, R. M., O'Day, E. B., Swee, M. B., Horenstein, A., & Heimberg, R. G. (2021). Cognitive behavioral therapy for social anxiety disorder: Predictors of treatment outcome in a quasi-naturalistic setting. *Behavior Therapy, 52*(2), 465–477. https://doi.org/10.1016/j.beth.2020.06.002

Cairney, J., McCabe, L., Veldhuizen, S., Corna, L. M., Streiner, D., & Herrmann, N. (2007). Epidemiology of social phobia in later life. *American Journal of Geriatric Psychiatry, 15*(3), 224–233. https://doi.org/10.1097/01.JGP.0000235702.77245.46

Calamaras, M. R., Tully, E. C., Tone, E. B., Price, M., & Anderson, P. L. (2015). Evaluating changes in judgmental biases as mechanisms of cognitive-behavioral therapy for social anxiety disorder. *Behaviour Research and Therapy, 71*, 139–149. https://doi.org/10.1016/j.brat.2015.06.006

Caldiroli, A., Capuzzi, E., Tagliabue, I., Ledda, L., Clerici, M., & Buoli, M. (2023). New frontiers in the pharmacological treatment of social anxiety disorder in adults: An up-to-date comprehensive overview. *Expert Opinion on Pharmacotherapy, 24*(2), 207–219. https://doi.org/10.1080/14656566.2022.2159373

Chambless, D. L., & Hope, D. A. (1996). Cognitive approaches to the psychopathology and treatment of social phobia. In P. M. Salkovskis (Ed.), *Frontiers of cognitive therapy* (pp. 345–382). Guilford Press.

Chambless, D. L., Tran, G. Q., & Glass, C. R. (1997). Predictors of response to cognitive-behavioral group therapy for social phobia. *Journal of Anxiety Disorders, 11*(3), 221–240. https://doi.org/10.1016/S0887-6185(97)00008-X

Chiu, K., Clark, D. M., & Leigh, E. (2021). Cognitive predictors of adolescent social anxiety. *Behaviour Research and Therapy, 137*, 103801. https://doi.org/10.1016/j.brat.2020.103801

Chorpita, B. F. (2007). *Modular cognitive-behavioral therapy for childhood anxiety disorders*. Guilford Press.

Chowdhury, N., & Khandoker, A. H. (2023). The gold-standard treatment for social anxiety disorder: A roadmap for the future. *Frontiers in Psychology, 13*, 1070975. https://doi.org/10.3389/fpsyg.2022.1070975

Choy, Y., Schneier, F. R., Heimberg, R. G., Oh, K.-S., & Liebowitz, M. R. (2008). Features of the offensive subtype of Taijin-Kyofu-Sho in US and Korean patients with DSM-IV social anxiety disorder. *Depression and Anxiety, 25*(3), 230–240. https://doi.org/10.1002/da.20295

Clark, D. M. (2001). A cognitive perspective on social phobia. In W. R. Crozier & L. E. Alden (Eds.), *International handbook of social anxiety: Concepts, research and interventions relating to the self and shyness* (pp. 405–430). John Wiley & Sons.

Clark, D. M., Ehlers, A., Hackmann, A., McManus, F., Fennell, M., Grey, N., Waddington, L., & Wild, J. (2006). Cognitive therapy versus exposure and applied relaxation in social phobia: A randomized controlled trial. *Journal of Consulting and Clinical Psychology, 74*(3), 568–578. https://doi.org/10.1037/0022-006X.74.3.568

Clark, D. M., & Wells, A. (1995). A cognitive model of social phobia. In R. G. Heimberg, M. R. Liebowitz, D. A. Hope, & F. R. Schneier (Eds.), *Social phobia: Diagnosis, assessment, and treatment* (pp. 69–93). Guilford Press.

Clark, D. M., Wild, J., Warnock-Parkes, E., Stott, R., Grey, N., Thew, G., & Ehlers, A. (2023). More than doubling the clinical benefit of each hour of therapist time: A randomised controlled trial of internet cognitive therapy for social anxiety disorder. *Psychological Medicine, 53*(11), 5022–5032. https://doi.org/10.1017/S0033291722002008

Colhoun, H., Kannis-Dymand, L., Rudge, M., Le Compte, D., O'Flaherty, S. J., Gilbert, C., Jones, M., Harrow, S.-E., Chambers, R., Woolcock, C., Macleod, J., Lovell, G. P., & Bell, C. (2021). Effectiveness of group cognitive therapy for social anxiety disorder in routine care. *Behaviour Change, 38*(2), 60–72. https://doi.org/10.1017/bec.2020.19

Conklin, L. R., Curreri, A. J., Farchione, T. J., & Barlow, D. H. (2021). Homework compliance and quality in cognitive behavioral therapies for anxiety disorders and obsessive-compulsive disorder. *Behavior Therapy, 52*(4), 1008–1018. https://doi.org/10.1016/j.beth.2021.01.001

Connor, K. M., Davidson, J. R., Churchill, L. E., Sherwood, A., Foa, E., & Weisler, R. H. (2000). Psychometric properties of the Social Phobia Inventory (SPIN): New self-rating scale. *British Journal of Psychiatry, 176*(4), 379–386. https://doi.org/10.1192/bjp.176.4.379

Cougle, J. R., Mueller, N. E., McDermott, K. A., Wilver, N. L., Carlton, C. N., & Okey, S. A. (2020). Text message safety behavior reduction for social anxiety: A randomized controlled trial. *Journal of Consulting and Clinical Psychology, 88*(5), 445–454. https://doi.org/10.1037/ccp0000494

Craske, M. G., & Mystkowski, J. L. (2006). Exposure therapy and extinction: Clinical studies. In M. G. Craske, D. Hermans, & D. Vansteenwegen (Eds.), *Fear and learning: From basic processes to clinical implications* (pp. 217–233). American Psychological Association. https://doi.org/10.1037/11474-011

Craske, M. G., Treanor, M., Conway, C. C., Zbozinek, T., & Vervliet, B. (2014). Maximizing exposure therapy: An inhibitory learning approach. *Behaviour Research and Therapy, 58*, 10–23. https://doi.org/10.1016/j.brat.2014.04.006

Cuming, S., Rapee, R. M., Kemp, N., Abbott, M. J., Peters, L., & Gaston, J. E. (2009). A self-report measure of subtle avoidance and safety behaviors relevant to social anxiety: Development and psychometric properties. *Journal of Anxiety Disorders, 23*(7), 879–883. https://doi.org/10.1016/j.janxdis.2009.05.002

Dabas, G., Rowa, K., Milosevic, I., Moscovitch, D. A., & McCabe, R. E. (2023). The impact of particular safety behaviours on perceived likeability and authenticity during interpersonal interactions in social anxiety disorder. *Behavioural and Cognitive Psychotherapy, 51*(1), 46–60. https://doi.org/10.1017/S1352465822000492

Davidson, J. R., Miner, C. M., De Veaugh-Geiss, J., Tupler, L. A., Colket, J. T., & Potts, N. L. (1997). The Brief Social Phobia Scale: A psychometric evaluation. *Psychological Medicine, 27*(1), 161–166. https://doi.org/10.1017/S0033291796004217

Davidson, J. R., Potts, N. L., Richichi, E. A., Ford, S. M., Krishnan, K. R., Smith, R. D., & Wilson, W. (1991). The Brief Social Phobia Scale. *Journal of Clinical Psychiatry, 52*(Suppl.), 48–51.

Devins, G. M., Binik, Y. M., Hutchinson, T. A., Hollomby, D. J., Barré, P. E., & Guttmann, R. D. (1983). The emotional impact of end-stage renal disease: Importance of patients' perception of intrusiveness and control. *International Journal of Psychiatry in Medicine, 13*(4), 327–343. https://doi.org/10.2190/5DCP-25BV-U1G9-9G7C

Edinoff, A. N., Nix, C. A., Hollier, J., Sagrera, C. E., Delacroix, B. M., Abubakar, T., Cornett, E. M., Kaye, A. M., & Kaye, A. D. (2021). Benzodiazepines: Uses, dangers, and clinical considerations. *Neurology International, 13*, 594–607. https://doi.org/10.3390/neurolint13040059

Eisen, A. R., & Engler, L. B. (2007). *Helping your socially vulnerable child: What to do when your child is shy, socially anxious, withdrawn, or bullied.* New Harbinger Publications.

Erwin, B. A., Heimberg, R. G., Juster, H., & Mindlin, M. (2002). Comorbid anxiety and mood disorders among persons with social anxiety disorder. *Behaviour Research and Therapy, 40*(1), 19–35. https://doi.org/10.1016/S0005-7967(00)00114-5

Erwin, B. A., Heimberg, R. G., Schneier, F. R., & Liebowitz, M. R. (2003). Anger experience and expression in social anxiety disorder: Pretreatment profile and predictors of attrition and response to cognitive-behavioral treatment. *Behavior Therapy, 34*(3), 331–350. https://doi.org/10.1016/S0005-7894(03)80004-7

Fang, A., Sawyer, A. T., Asnaani, A., & Hofmann, S. (2013). Social mishap exposures for social anxiety disorder: An important treatment ingredient. *Cognitive and Behavioral Practice, 20*(2), 213–220. https://doi.org/10.1016/j.cbpra.2012.05.003

Federoff, I. C., & Taylor, S. (2001). Psychological and pharmacological treatments of social phobia: A meta-analysis. *Journal of Clinical Psychopharmacology, 21*(3), 311-324. https://doi.org/10.1097/00004714-200106000-00011

Feske, U., & Chambless, D. L. (1995). Cognitive behavioral versus exposure only treatment for social phobia: A meta-analysis. *Behavior Therapy, 26*(4), 695-720. https://doi.org/10.1016/S0005-7894(05)80040-1

Foa, E. B., & Kozak, M. J. (1986). Emotional processing of fear: Exposure to corrective information. *Psychological Bulletin, 99*(1), 20-35. https://doi.org/10.1037/0033-2909.99.1.20

Gavric, D., Cameron, D., Waechter, S., Moscovitch, D. A., McCabe, R. E., & Rowa, K. (2023). Just do something: An experimental investigation of brief interventions for reducing the negative impact of post-event processing in social anxiety disorder. *Journal of Anxiety Disorders, 98*, 102744. https://doi.org/10.2139/ssrn.4129952

Gladstone, G. L., Parker, G. B., & Malhi, G. S. (2006). Do bullied children become anxious and depressed adults? A cross-sectional investigation of the correlates of bullying and anxious depression. *Journal of Nervous and Mental Disease, 194*(3), 201-208. https://doi.org/10.1097/01.nmd.0000202491.99719.c3

Goldin, P. R., Ziv, M., Jazaieri, H., Werner, K., Kraemer, H., Heimberg, R. G., & Gross, J. J. (2012). Cognitive reappraisal self-efficacy mediates the effects of individual cognitive-behavioral therapy for social anxiety disorder. *Journal of Consulting and Clinical Psychology, 80*(6), 1034-1040. https://doi.org/10.1037/a0028555

Gould, R. A., Buckminster, S., Pollack, M. H., Otto, M. W., & Yap, L. (1997). Cognitive-behavioral and pharmacological treatment for social phobia: A meta-analysis. *Clinical Psychology: Science and Practice, 4*(4), 291-306. https://doi.org/10.1111/j.1468-2850.1997.tb00123.x

Gregory, B., Peters, L., Abbott, M. J., Gaston, J. E., & Rapee, R. M. (2015). Relationships between probability estimates, cost estimates, and social anxiety during CBT for social anxiety disorder. *Cognitive Therapy and Research, 39*, 636-645. https://doi.org/10.1007/s10608-015-9692-6

Gregory, B., Wong, Q. J., Marker, C. D., & Peters, L. (2018). Maladaptive self-beliefs during cognitive behavioural therapy for social anxiety disorder: A test of temporal precedence. *Cognitive Therapy and Research, 42*(3), 261-272. https://doi.org/10.1007/s10608-017-9882-5

Guastella, A. J., Richardson, R., Lovibond, P. F., Rapee, R. M., Gaston, J. E., Mitchell, P., & Dadds, M. R. (2008). A randomized controlled trial of d-cycloserine enhancement of exposure therapy for social anxiety disorder. *Biological Psychiatry, 63*(6), 544-549. https://doi.org/10.1016/j.biopsych.2007.11.011

Guo, S., Deng, W., Wang, H., Liu, J., Liu, X., Yang, X., He, C., Zhang, Q., Liu, B., Dong, X., Yang, Z., Li, Z., & Li, X. (2021). The efficacy of internet-based cognitive behavioural therapy for social anxiety disorder: A systematic review and meta-analysis. *Clinical Psychology & Psychotherapy, 28*(3), 656-668. https://doi.org/10.1002/cpp.2528

Hambrick, J. P., Rodebaugh, T. L., Balsis, S., Woods, C. M., Mendez, J. L., & Heimberg, R. G. (2010). Cross-ethnic measurement equivalence of measures of depression, social anxiety, and worry. *Assessment, 17*(2), 155-171. https://doi.org/10.1177/1073191109350158

Hayes, S. A., Hope, D. A., & Heimberg, R. G. (2008). The pattern of subjective anxiety during in-session exposures over the course of cognitive-behavioral therapy for clients with social anxiety disorder. *Behavior Therapy, 39*(3), 286-299. https://doi.org/10.1016/j.beth.2007.09.001

Heimberg, R. G., & Becker, R. E. (2002). *Cognitive-behavioral group therapy for social phobia: Basic mechanisms and clinical strategies*. Guilford Press.

Heimberg, R. G., Brozovich, F. A., & Rapee, R. M. (2010). A cognitive behavioral model of social anxiety disorder: Update and extension. In S. G. Hofmann & P. M. DiBartolo (Eds.), *Social anxiety: Clinical, developmental, and social perspectives* (2nd ed., pp. 395-422). Elsevier Academic Press.

Heimberg, R. G., Brozovich, F. A., & Rapee, R. M. (2014). A cognitive-behavioral model of social anxiety disorder. In S. G. Hofmann & P. M. DiBartolo (Eds.), *Social anxiety: Clinical, developmental, and social perspectives* (3rd ed., pp. 705–728). Elsevier Academic Press. https://doi.org/10.1016/B978-0-12-394427-6.00024-8

Heimberg, R. G., Horner, K. J., Juster, H. R., Safren, S. A., Brown, E. J., Schneier, F. R., & Liebowitz, M. R. (1999). Psychometric properties of the Liebowitz Social Anxiety Scale. *Psychological Medicine, 29*(1), 199–212. https://doi.org/10.1017/S0033291 798007879

Heimberg, R. G., Makris, G. S., Juster, H. R., Ost, L.-G., & Rapee, R. M. (1997). Social phobia: A preliminary cross-national comparison. *Depression and Anxiety, 5*(3), 130–133. https://doi.org/10.1002/(SICI)1520-6394(1997)5:3<130::AID-DA4>3.0.CO;2-I

Henderson, L., & Zimbardo, P. (2010). Shyness, social anxiety, and social anxiety disorder. In S. G. Hofmann & P. M. DiBartolo (Eds.), *Social anxiety: Clinical, developmental, and social perspectives* (2nd ed., pp. 65–92). Elsevier Academic Press.

Hirshfeld-Becker, D., Micco, J. A., Wang, C. H., & Henin, A. (2014). Behavioral inhibition: A discrete precursor to social anxiety disorder? In J. W. Weeks (Ed.), *The Wiley Blackwell handbook of social anxiety disorder* (pp. 133–158). Wiley Blackwell. https://doi.org/10.1002/9781118653920.ch7

Hofmann, S. G. (2007). Cognitive factors that maintain social anxiety disorder: A comprehensive model and its treatment implications. *Cognitive Behaviour Therapy, 36*(4), 193–209. https://doi.org/10.1080/16506070701421313

Hofmann, S. G. (2023). *CBT for social anxiety: Simple skills for overcoming fear and enjoying people*. New Harbinger Publications.

Hofmann, S. G., Asnaani, A., & Hinton, D. E. (2010). Cultural aspects in social anxiety and social anxiety disorder. *Depression and Anxiety, 27*(12), 1117–1127. https://doi.org/10.1002/da.20759

Hofmann, S. G., Meuret, A. E., Smits, J. A., Simon, N. M., Pollack, M. H., Eisenmenger, K., Shiekh, M., & Otto, M. W. (2006). Augmentation of exposure therapy with d-cycloserine for social anxiety disorder. *Archives of General Psychiatry, 63*(3), 298–304. https://doi.org/10.1001/archpsyc.63.3.298

Hope, D. A., Heimberg, R. G., & Turk, C. L. (2019). *Managing social anxiety: A cognitive behavioral therapy approach* (therapist guide; 3rd ed.). Oxford University Press. https://doi.org/10.1093/med-psych/9780190247591.001.0001

Hudson, J. L., & Rapee, R. M. (2001). Parent–child interactions and anxiety disorders: An observational study. *Behaviour Research and Therapy, 39*(12), 1411–1427. https://doi.org/10.1016/S0005-7967(00)00107-8

Jankowska, M. (2019). Cultural modifications of cognitive behavioural treatment of social anxiety among culturally diverse clients: A systematic literature review. *Cognitive Behaviour Therapist, 12*, 25. https://doi.org/10.1017/S1754470X18000211

Jefferies, P., & Ungar, M. (2020). Social anxiety in young people: A prevalence study in seven countries. *PLOS ONE, 15*(9), e0239133. https://doi.org/10.1371/journal.pone.0239133

Kampmann, I. L., Emmelkamp, P. M. G., & Morina, N. (2016). Meta-analysis of technology-assisted interventions for social anxiety disorder. *Journal of Anxiety Disorders, 42*, 71–84. https://doi.org/10.1016/j.janxdis.2016.06.007

Katzman, M. A., Bleau, P., Blier, P., Chokka, P., Kjernisted, K., & Van Ameringen, M. (2014). Canadian clinical practice guidelines for the management of anxiety, posttraumatic stress and obsessive-compulsive disorders. *BMC Psychiatry, 14*, 83. https://doi.org/10.1186/1471-244X-14-S1-S1

Kearney, C. A. (2005). *Social anxiety and social phobia in youth: Characteristics, assessment, and psychological treatment*. Springer. https://doi.org/10.1007/b99417

Keller, M. B. (2003). The lifelong course of social anxiety disorder: A clinical perspective. *Acta Psychiatrica Scandinavica, 108*(s417), 85–94. https://doi.org/10.1034/j.1600-0447.108.s417.6.x

Kessler, R. C., Berglund, P., Demler, O., Jin, R., Merikangas, K. R., & Walters, E. E. (2005). Lifetime prevalence and age-of-onset distributions of DSM-IV disorders in the National Comorbidity Survey Replication. *Archives of General Psychiatry, 62*(6), 593–602. https://doi.org/10.1001/archpsyc.62.6.593

Kim, J., Rapee, R. M., & Gaston, J. E. (2008). Symptoms of offensive type Taijin-Kyofusho among Australian social phobics. *Depression and Anxiety, 25*(7), 601–608. https://doi.org/10.1002/da.20345

Kindred, R., & Bates, G. W. (2023). The influence of the COVID-19 pandemic on social anxiety: A systematic review. *International Journal of Environmental Research and Public Health, 20*(3), 2362. https://doi.org/10.3390/ijerph20032362

Kivity, Y., Strauss, A. Y., Elizur, J., Weiss, M., Cohen, L., & Huppert, J. D. (2022). Patterns of alliance development in cognitive behavioral therapy versus attention bias modification for social anxiety disorder: Sawtooth patterns and sudden gains. *Journal of Clinical Psychology, 78*(2), 122–136. https://doi.org/10.1002/jclp.23219

Kocovski, N. L., Fleming, J. E., Hawley, L. L., Huta, V., & Antony, M. M. (2013). Mindfulness and acceptance-based group therapy versus traditional cognitive behavioral group therapy for social anxiety disorder: A randomized controlled trial. *Behaviour Research and Therapy, 51*(12), 889–898. https://doi.org/10.1016/j.brat.2013.10.007

Koyuncu, A., Ertekin, E., Deveci, E., Ertekin, B. A., Yüksel, Ç., Çelebi, F., Binbay, Z., Demir, E. Y., & Tükel, R. (2015). Age of onset in social anxiety disorder: Relation to clinical variables and major depression comorbidity. *Annals of Clinical Psychiatry, 27*(2), 84–89.

Koyuncu, A., İnce, E., Ertekin, E., & Tükel, R. (2019). Comorbidity in social anxiety disorder: Diagnostic and therapeutic challenges. *Drugs in Context, 8*, 212573. https://doi.org/10.7573/dic.212573

Kushner, M. G., Krueger, R., Frye, B., & Peterson, J. (2008). Epidemiological perspectives on co-occurring anxiety disorder and substance use disorder. In S. H. Stewart & P. J. Conrod (Eds.), *Anxiety and substance use disorders: The vicious cycle of comorbidity* (pp. 3–17). Springer.

Landkroon, E., Salemink, E., Meyerbröker, K., Barzilay, S., Kalanthroff, E., Huppert, J. D., & Engelhard, I. M. (2022). The effect of imagery rescripting on prospective mental imagery of a feared social situation. *Journal of Behavior Therapy and Experimental Psychiatry, 77*, 101764. https://doi.org/10.1016/j.jbtep.2022.101764

Laposa, J. M., & Rector, N. A. (2023). The impact of group feedback on self-perceptions following videotape exposure in CBT for social anxiety disorder. *Behavior Modification, 47*(3), 573–589. https://doi.org/10.1177/01454455221118349

Ledley, D. R., & Heimberg, R. G. (2005). Social anxiety disorder. In M. M. Antony, D. R. Ledley, & R. G. Heimberg (Eds.), *Improving outcomes and preventing relapse in cognitive-behavorial therapy* (pp. 38–76). Guilford Press.

LeMoult, J., Rowa, K., Antony, M., Chudzik, S., & McCabe, R. (2014). Effect of comorbid depression on cognitive behavioural group therapy for social anxiety disorder. *Behaviour Change, 31*(1), 53–64. https://doi.org/10.1017/bec.2013.32

Lenton-Brym, A. P., Rogojanski, J., Hood, H. K., Vorstenbosch, V., McCabe, R. E., & Antony, M. M. (2020). Development and validation of the Ryerson Social Anxiety Scales (RSAS). *Anxiety, Stress, and Coping, 33*(6), 642–660. https://doi.org/10.1080/10615806.2020.1771137

Leung, A. W., & Heimberg, R. G. (1996). Homework compliance, perceptions of control, and outcome of cognitive-behavioral treatment of social phobia. *Behaviour Research and Therapy, 34*(5–6), 423–432. https://doi.org/10.1016/0005-7967(96)00014-9

Liebowitz, M. R. (1987). Social phobia. *Modern Problems of Pharmacopsychiatry, 22*, 141–173. https://doi.org/10.1159/000414022

Liebowitz, M. R., Heimberg, R. G., Schneier, F. R., Hope, D. A., Davies, S., Holt, C. S., Goetz, D., Juster, H. R., Lin, S. H., Bruch, M. A., Marshall, R. D., & Klein, D. F. (1999). Cognitive-behavioral group therapy versus phenelzine in social phobia: Long-term outcome. *Depression and Anxiety, 10*(3), 89–98. https://doi.org/10.1002/(SICI)1520-6394(1999)10:3<89::AID-DA1>3.0.CO;2-5

Lloyd, J., & Marczak, M. (2022). Imagery rescripting and negative self-imagery in social anxiety disorder: A systematic literature review. *Behavioural and Cognitive Psychotherapy, 50*(3), 280–297. https://doi.org/10.1017/S135246582200008X

MacKenzie, M. B., & Fowler, K. F. (2013). Social anxiety disorder in the Canadian population: Exploring gender differences in sociodemographic profile. *Journal of Anxiety Disorders, 27*(4), 427–434. https://doi.org/10.1016/j.janxdis.2013.05.006

Mattick, R. P., & Clarke, J. C. (1998). Development and validation of measures of social phobia scrutiny fear and social interaction anxiety. *Behaviour Research and Therapy, 36*(4), 455–470. https://doi.org/10.1016/S0005-7967(97)10031-6

Mayo-Wilson, E., Dias, S., Mavranezouli, I., Kew, K., Clark, D. M., Ades, A. E., & Pilling, S. (2014). Psychological and pharmacological interventions for social anxiety disorder in adults: A systematic review and network meta-analysis. *Lancet Psychiatry, 1*(5), 368–376. https://doi.org/10.1016/S2215-0366(14)70329-3

McCabe, R. E., Antony, M. M., Summerfeldt, L. J., Liss, A., & Swinson, R. P. (2003). Preliminary examination of the relationship between anxiety disorders in adults and self-reported history of teasing or bullying experiences. *Cognitive Behaviour Therapy, 32*(4), 187–193. https://doi.org/10.1080/16506070310005051

McCabe, R. E., Milosevic, I., Rowa, K., Shnaider, P., Key, B., Antony, M. M., & the DART Working Group. (2021). *Diagnostic Assessment Research Tool (DART), Version 4.0* [Unpublished instrument]. St. Jospeh's Healthcare/McMaster University.

McEvoy, P. M., Saulsman, L. M., & Rapee, R. M. (2018). *Imagery-enhanced CBT for social anxiety disorder*. Guilford Press.

McIndoo, C. C., & Hopko, D. R. (2014). Cognitive-behavioral therapy for an Arab college student with social phobia and depression. *Clinical Case Studies, 13*(2), 128–145. https://doi.org/10.1177/1534650113504132

McKay, M., Davis, M, & Fanning, P. (2018). *Messages: The communications skills book* (4th ed.). New Harbinger Publications.

McConnell, B., Laugeson, N., and the Anxiety Treatment and Research Clinic. (2017). Cognitive behavioural therapy for social anxiety disorder. St. Joseph's Healthcare, Hamilton, Canada.

Meidlinger, P. C., & Hope, D. A. (2014). Diversity considerations in the assessment and treatment of social anxiety disorder. In J. W. Weeks (Ed.), *The Wiley Blackwell handbook of social anxiety disorder* (pp. 223–246). Wiley Blackwell. https://doi.org/10.1002/9781118653920.ch11

Miller, W. R., & Rollnick, S. (2023). *Motivational interviewing: Helping people change and grow* (4th ed.). Guilford Press.

Milosevic, I., Cameron, D. H., Milanovic, M., McCabe, R. E., & Rowa, K. (2022). Face-to-face versus video teleconference group cognitive behavioural therapy for anxiety and related disorders: A preliminary comparison. *Canadian Journal of Psychiatry, 67*(5), 391–402. https://doi.org/10.1177/07067437211027319

Mohlman, J., Gorenstein, E. E., Kleber, M., de Jesus, M., Gorman, J. M., & Papp, L. A. (2003). Standard and enhanced cognitive-behavior therapy for late-life generalized anxiety disorder: Two pilot investigations. *American Journal of Geriatric Psychiatry, 11*(1), 24–32. https://doi.org/10.1097/00019442-200301000-00005

Moradi, B. (2013). Discrimination, objectification, and dehumanization: Toward a pantheoretical framework. In S. J. Gervais (Ed.), *Objectification and (de)humanization: 60th Nebraska Symposium on Motivation* (pp. 153–181). Springer Science.

Mörtberg, E., Clark, D. M., Sundin, Ö., & Åberg Wistedt, A. (2007). Intensive group cognitive treatment and individual cognitive therapy vs. treatment as usual in social phobia: A randomized controlled trial. *Acta Psychiatrica Scandinavica, 115*(2), 142–154.

Mörtberg, E., Hoffart, A., Boecking, B., & Clark, D. M. (2015). Shifting the focus of one's attention mediates improvement in cognitive therapy for social anxiety disorder. *Behavioural and Cognitive Psychotherapy, 43*(1), 63–73. https://doi.org/10.1017/S1352465813000738

Moscovitch, D. A. (2009). What is the core fear in social phobia? A new model to facilitate individualized case conceptualization and treatment. *Cognitive and Behavioral Practice, 16*(2), 123-134. https://doi.org/10.1016/j.cbpra.2008.04.002

Moscovitch, D. A., Antony, M. M., & Swinson, R. P. (2009). Exposure-based treatments for anxiety disorders: Theory and process. In M. M. Antony & M. B. Stein (Eds.), *Oxford handbook of anxiety and related disorders* (pp. 461-475). Oxford University Press.

Moscovitch, D. A., Gavric, D. L., Merrifield, C., Bielak, T., & Moscovitch, M. (2011). Retrieval properties of negative vs. positive mental images and autobiographical memories in social anxiety: Outcomes with a new measure. *Behaviour Research and Therapy, 49*(8), 505-517.

Moscovitch, D. A., & Huyder, V. (2011). The negative self-portrayal scale: Development, validation, and application to social anxiety. *Behavior Therapy, 42*(2), 183-196. https://doi.org/10.1016/j.beth.2010.04.007

Moscovitch, D. A., Rowa, K., Paulitzki, J. R., Antony, M. M., McCabe, R. E. (2015). What if I appear boring, anxious, or unattractive? Validation and treatment sensitivity of the Negative Self Portrayal Scale in clinical samples. *Cognitive Therapy and Research, 39*(2), 178-192. https://doi.org/10.1007/s10608-014-9645-5

Moscovitch, D. A., Rowa, K., Paulitzki, J. R., Ierullo, M. D., Chiang, B., Antony, M. M., & McCabe, R. E. (2013). Self-portrayal concerns and their relation to safety behaviors and negative affect in social anxiety disorder. *Behaviour Research and Therapy, 51*(8), 476-486. https://doi.org/10.1016/j.brat.2013.05.002

Neal, J. A., & Edelmann, R. J. (2003). The etiology of social phobia: Toward a developmental profile. *Clinical Psychology Review, 23*(6), 761-786. https://doi.org/10.1016/S0272-7358(03)00076-X

Orr, E. M. J., & Moscovitch, D. A. (2010). Learning to re-appraise the self during video feedback for social anxiety: Does depth of processing matter? *Behaviour Research and Therapy, 48*(8), 728-737. https://doi.org/10.1016/j.brat.2010.04.004

Otto, M. W., Pollack, M. H., Gould, R. A., Worthington, J. J., III, McArdle, E. T., Rosenbaum, J. F., & Heimberg, R. G. (2000). A comparison of the efficacy of clonazepam and cognitive-behavioral group therapy for the treatment of social phobia. *Journal of Anxiety Disorders, 14*(4), 345-358. https://doi.org/10.1016/S0887-6185(00)00027-X

Paterson, R. J. (2022). *The assertiveness workbook: How to express your ideas and stand up for yourself at work and in relationships* (2nd ed.). New Harbinger Publications.

Perera, S., Rowa, K., & McCabe, R. E. (2016). Post-event processing across multiple anxiety presentations: Is it specific to social anxiety disorder? *Behavioural and Cognitive Psychotherapy, 44*(5), 568-579. https://doi.org/10.1017/S1352465815000697

Peters, L., Romano, M., Byrow, Y., Gregory, B., McLellan, L. F., Brockveld, K., Baillie, A., Gaston, J., & Rapee, R. M. (2019). Motivational interviewing prior to cognitive behavioural treatment for social anxiety disorder: A randomised controlled trial. *Journal of Affective Disorders, 256*, 70-78. https://doi.org/10.1016/j.jad.2019.05.042

Peterson, R. A., & Reiss, S. (1993). *Anxiety Sensitivity Index revised test manual*. IDS Publishing Corporation.

Peyre, H., Barret, S., Landman, B., Blanco, C., Ellul, P., Limosin, F., Hoertel, N., & Delorme, R. (2022). Age of onset of social anxiety disorder and psychiatric and mental health outcomes: Results from a nationally representative study. *Journal of Affective Disorders, 309*, 252-258. https://doi.org/10.1016/j.jad.2022.04.149

Piccirillo, M. L., Taylor Dryman, M., & Heimberg, R. G. (2016). Safety behaviors in adults with social anxiety: Review and future directions. *Behavior Therapy, 47*(5), 675-687. https://doi.org/10.1016/j.beth.2015.11.005

Plasencia, M. L., Taylor, C. T., & Alden, L. E. (2016). Unmasking one's true self facilitates positive relational outcomes: Authenticity promotes social approach processes in social anxiety disorder. *Clinical Psychological Science, 4*(6), 1002-1014. https://doi.org/10.1177/2167702615622204

Price, M., & Anderson, P. L. (2012). Outcome expectancy as a predictor of treatment response in cognitive behavioral therapy for public speaking fears within social anxiety disorder. *Psychotherapy, 49*(2), 173-179. https://doi.org/10.1037/a0024734

Rachman, S. (1977). The conditioning theory of fear-acquisition: A critical examination. *Behaviour Research and Therapy, 15*(5), 375-387. https://doi.org/10.1016/0005-7967(77)90041-9

Rapee, R. M., & Heimberg, R. G. (1997). A cognitive-behavioral model of anxiety in social phobia. *Behaviour Research and Therapy, 35*(8), 741-756. https://doi.org/10.1016/S0005-7967(97)00022-3

Rapee, R. M., Spence, S. H., Cobham, V., Wignall, A., & Lyneham, H. (2022). *Helping your anxious child: A step-by-step guide for parents* (3rd ed.). New Harbinger Publications.

Rescorla, R. A. (2001). Experimental extinction. In R. R. Mowrer & S. B. Klein (Eds.), *Handbook of contemporary learning theories* (pp. 119-154). Lawrence Erlbaum Associates.

Riches, S., Hammond, N., Bianco, M., Fialho, C., & Acland, J. (2023). Adapting cognitive behaviour therapy for adults with autism: A lived experience-led consultation with specialist psychological therapists. *Cognitive Behaviour Therapist, 16*, e13. https://doi.org/10.1017/S1754470X23000053

Rogojanski, J., Hood, H. K., Vorstenbosch, V., & Antony, M. M. (2019). *Ryerson Social Anxiety Scales* [Unpublished scale]. Department of Psychology, Toronto Metropolitan University, Canada.

Romano, M., & Peters, L. (2021). The effect of motivational interviewing on ambivalence in social anxiety disorder. *Behavioural and Cognitive Psychotherapy, 49*(6), 684-695. https://doi.org/10.1017/S1352465821000138

Roth, D. A., Coles, M. E., & Heimberg, R. G. (2002). The relationship between memories for childhood teasing and anxiety and depression in adulthood. *Journal of Anxiety Disorders, 16*(2), 149-164. https://doi.org/10.1016/S0887-6185(01)00096-2

Rowa, K., Gavric, D., Stead, V., LeMoult, J., & McCabe, R. E. (2016). The pernicious effects of post-event processing in social anxiety disorder. *Journal of Experimental Psychopathology, 7*(4), 577-587. https://doi.org/10.5127/jep.056916

Rowa, K., Gifford, S., McCabe, R., Milosevic, I., Antony, M. M., & Purdon, C. (2014). Treatment fears in anxiety disorders: Development and validation of the Treatment Ambivalence Questionnaire. *Journal of Clinical Psychology, 70*(10), 979-993. https://doi.org/10.1002/jclp.22096

Rowa, K., Paulitzki, J. R., Ierullo, M. D., Chiang, B., Antony, M. M., McCabe, R. E., & Moscovitch, D. A. (2015). A false sense of security: Safety behaviors erode objective speech performance in individuals with social anxiety disorder. *Behavior Therapy, 46*(3), 304-314. https://doi.org/10.1016/j.beth.2014.11.004

Rozen, N., & Aderka, I. M. (2021). The effect of depression on treatment outcome in social anxiety disorder: An individual-level meta-analysis. *Cognitive Behaviour Therapy, 51*(3), 185-216. https://doi.org/10.1080/16506073.2021.1966089

Rytwinski, N. K., Fresco, D. M., Heimberg, R. G., Coles, M. E., Liebowitz, M. R., Cissell, S., Stein, M. B., & Hofmann, S. G. (2009). Screening for social anxiety disorder with the self-report version of the Liebowitz Social Anxiety Scale. *Depression and Anxiety, 26*(1), 34-38. https://doi.org/10.1002/da.20503

Safren, S. A., Heimberg, R. G., & Juster, H. R. (1997). Clients' expectancies and their relationship to pretreatment symptomatology and outcome of cognitive-behavioral group treatment for social phobia. *Journal of Consulting and Clinical Psychology, 65*(4), 694-698. https://doi.org/10.1037/0022-006X.65.4.694

Safren, S. A., & Pantalone, D. W. (2006). Social anxiety and barriers to resilience among lesbian, gay, and bisexual adolescents. In A. M. Omoto & H. S. Kurtzman (Eds.), *Sexual orientation and mental health: Examining identity and development in lesbian, gay, and bisexual people* (pp. 55-71). American Psychological Association. https://doi.org/10.1037/11261-003

Schneider, L. H., Pawluk, E. J., Milosevic, I., Shnaider, P., Rowa, K., Antony, M. M., Musielak, N., & McCabe, R. E. (2022). The Diagnostic Assessment Research Tool in action: A preliminary evaluation of a semistructured diagnostic interview for DSM-5 disorders. *Psychological Assessment, 34*(1), 21–29. https://doi.org/10.1037/pas0001059

Schreier, S. S., Heinrichs, N., Alden, L., Rapee, R. M., Hofmann, S. G., Chen, J., Oh, K. J., & Bögels, S. (2010). Social anxiety and social norms in individualistic and collectivistic countries. *Depression and Anxiety, 27*(12), 1128–1134. https://doi.org/10.1002/da.20746

Schuurmans, J., Comijs, H., Emmelkamp, P. M., Gundy, C. M., Weijnen, I., van den Hout, M., & van Dyck, R. (2006). A randomized, controlled trial of the effectiveness of cognitive-behavioral therapy and sertraline versus a waitlist control group for anxiety disorders in older adults. *American Journal of Geriatric Psychiatry, 14*(3), 255–263. https://doi.org/10.1097/01.JGP.0000196629.19634.00

Shannon, J. (2022). *The shyness and social anxiety workbook for teens: CBT and ACT skills to help you build social confidence* (2nd ed.). New Harbinger Publications.

Smits, J. A. J., Pollack, M. H., Rosenfield, D., Otto, M. W., Dowd, S., Carpenter, J., Dutcher, C. D., Lewis, E. M., Witcraft, S. M., Papini, S., Curtiss, J., Andrews, L., Kind, S., Conroy, K., & Hofmann, S. G. (2020). Dose timing of d-cycloserine to augment exposure therapy for social anxiety disorder: A randomized clinical trial. *JAMA Network Open, 3*(6), e206777.

Solmi, M., Radua, J., Olivola, M., Croce, E., Soaddo, L., Salazar de Pablo, G., Shin, J., Kirkbride, J. B., Jones, P., Kim, J., Kim, J. Y., Carvalho, A. F., Seeman, M. V., Correll, C. U., & Fusar-Poli, P. (2022). Age at onset of mental disorders worldwide: Large-scale meta-analysis of 192 epidemiological studies. *Molecular Psychiatry, 27*, 281–295.

Stangier, U., Heidenreich, T., & Schermelleh-Engel, K. (2006). Safety behaviors and social performance in patients with generalized social phobia. *Journal of Cognitive Psychotherapy, 20*(1), 17–31. https://doi.org/10.1891/jcop.20.1.17

Stangier, U., Schramm, E., Heidenreich, T., Berger, M., & Clark, D. M. (2011). Cognitive therapy vs interpersonal psychotherapy in social anxiety disorder: A randomized controlled trial. *Archives of General Psychiatry, 68*(7), 692–700. https://doi.org/10.1001/archgenpsychiatry.2011.67

Stein, D. J., Kawakami, N., de Girolamo, G., & Lépine, J. (2018). Social anxiety disorder. In K. M. Scott, P. de Jonge, D. J. Stein, & R. C. Kessler (Eds.), *Mental disorders around the world: Facts and figures from the WHO world mental health surveys* (pp. 120–133). Cambridge University Press.

Stein, M. B., Fuetsch, M., Müller, N., Höfler, M., Lieb, R., & Wittchen, H. U. (2001). Social anxiety disorder and the risk of depression: A prospective community study of adolescents and young adults. *Archives of General Psychiatry, 58*(3), 251–256. https://doi.org/10.1001/archpsyc.58.3.251

Stopa L. (2009). Why is the self important in understanding and treating social phobia? *Cognitive Behaviour Therapy, 38*(Suppl. 1), 48–54.

Suh, D. E., Chang, K.-A., Hwang, J. U., & Kwon, J.-H. (2020). Prevalence and features of spontaneous recurrent images in social anxiety disorder: Findings from a Korean community sample. *Behavioural and Cognitive Psychotherapy, 48*(2), 172–184. https://doi.org/10.1017/S135246581900064X

Taube-Schiff, M., Suvak, M. K., Antony, M. M., Bieling, P. J., & McCabe, R. E. (2007). Group cohesion in cognitive-behavioral group therapy for social phobia. *Behaviour Research and Therapy, 45*(4), 687–698. https://doi.org/10.1016/j.brat.2006.06.004

Taylor, S. (1996). Meta-analysis of cognitive-behavioral treatments for social phobia. *Journal of Behavior Therapy and Experimental Psychiatry, 27*(1), 1–9. https://doi.org/10.1016/0005-7916(95)00058-5

Taylor, S., Zvolensky, M. J., Cox, B. J., Deacon, B., Heimberg, R. G., Ledley, D. R., Abramowitz, J. S., Holaway, R. M., Sandin, B., Stewart, S. H., Coles, M., Eng, W., Daly, E. S., Arrindell, W. A., Bouvard, M., & Cardenas, S. J. (2007). Robust dimensions of anxiety sensitivity: Development and initial validation of the Anxiety Sensitivity Index-3. *Psychological Assessment, 19*(2), 176–188.

Tolin, D. F. (2019). Inhibitory learning for anxiety-related disorders. *Cognitive and Behavioral Practice, 26*(1), 225–236. https://doi.org/10.1016/j.cbpra.2018.07.008

Toyokawa, T., & Nedate, K. (1996). Application of cognitive behavior therapy to interpersonal problems: A case study of a Japanese female client. *Cognitive and Behavioral Practice, 3*(2), 289–302. https://doi.org/10.1016/S1077-7229(96)80019-8

Tsekova, V., Lenton-Brym, A. P., Rogojanski, J., Hood, H. K., Vorstenbosch, V., McCabe, R. E., & Antony, M. M. (2021). Psychometric properties of the Ryerson Social Anxiety Scales in individuals with social anxiety disorder. *Anxiety, Stress, and Coping, 34*(5), 559–570. https://doi.org/10.1080/10615806.2020.1870108

van Dis, E. A. M., van Veen, S. C., Hagenaars, M. A., Batelaan, N. M., Bockting, C. L. H., van den Heuvel, R. M., Cuijpers, P., & Engelhard, I. M. (2020). Long-term outcomes of cognitive behavioral therapy for anxiety-related disorders: A systematic review and meta-analysis. *JAMA Psychiatry, 77*(3), 265–273. https://doi.org/10.1001/jamapsychiatry.2019.3986

Warnock-Parkes, E., Wild, J., Stott, R., Grey, N., Ehlers, A., & Clark, D. M. (2017). Seeing is believing: Using video feedback in cognitive therapy for social anxiety disorder. *Cognitive and Behavioral Practice, 24*(2), 245–255. https://doi.org/10.1016/j.cbpra.2016.03.007

Warnock-Parkes, E., Wild, J., Thew, G. R., Kerr, A., Grey, N., Stott, R., Ehlers, A., & Clark, D. M. (2020). Treating social anxiety disorder remotely with cognitive therapy. *Cognitive Behaviour Therapist, 13*, e30. https://doi.org/10.1017/S1754470X2000032X

Weeks, J. W., Heimberg, R. G., & Rodebaugh, T. L. (2008). The fear of positive evaluation scale: Assessing a proposed cognitive component of social anxiety. *Journal of Anxiety Disorders, 22*(1), 44–55. https://doi.org/10.1016/j.janxdis.2007.08.002

Weisman, J. S., & Rodebaugh, T. L. (2018). Exposure therapy augmentation: A review and extension of techniques informed by an inhibitory learning approach. *Clinical Psychology Review, 59*, 41–51. https://doi.org/10.1016/j.cpr.2017.10.010

Weiss, B. J., Singh, J. S., & Hope, D. A. (2011). Cognitive-behavioral therapy for immigrants presenting with social anxiety disorder: Two case studies. *Clinical Case Studies, 10*(4), 324–342. https://doi.org/10.1177/1534650111420706

Weissman, M. M., Bland, R. C., Canino, G. J., Greenwald, S., Lee, C. K., Newman, S. C., Rubio-Stipec, M., & Wickramaratne, P. J. (1996). The cross-national epidemiology of social phobia. *International Clinical Psychopharmacology, 11*(3), 9–14. https://doi.org/10.1097/00004850-199606003-00003

Westra, H. A., & Dozois, D. J. A. (2006). Preparing clients for cognitive behavioral therapy: A randomized pilot study of motivational interviewing for anxiety. *Cognitive Therapy and Research, 30*(4), 481–498. https://doi.org/10.1007/s10608-006-9016-y

Wheaton, M. G., Deacon, B. J., McGrath, P. B., Berman, N. C., & Abramowitz, J. S. (2012). Dimensions of anxiety sensitivity in the anxiety disorders: Evaluation of the ASI-3. *Journal of Anxiety Disorders, 26*(3), 401–408. https://doi.org/10.1016/j.janxdis.2012.01.002

Wild, J., & Clark, D. M. (2011). Imagery rescripting of early traumatic memories in social phobia. *Cognitive and Behavioral Practice, 18*(4), 433–443. https://doi.org/10.1016/j.cbpra.2011.03.002

Wild, J., Warnock-Parkes, E., Stott, R., Kwok, A. P. L., Lissillour Chan, M. H., Powell, C. L. Y. M., Leung, P. W. L., Clark, D. M., & Thew, G. R. (2023). Video feedback to update negative self-perceptions in social anxiety disorder: A comparison of internet-delivered vs face-to-face cognitive therapy formats. *Journal of Affective Disorders, 331*, 139–144.

Wilson, G. A., Malivoire, B. L., Cassin, S. E., & Antony, M. M. (2023). A mixed methods investigation of reasons underlying fear of positive evaluation. *Clinical Psychology and Psychotherapy, 30*(2), 473–485. https://doi.org/10.1002/cpp.2818

Woody, S. R., & Adessky, R. S. (2002). Therapeutic alliance, group cohesion, and homework compliance during cognitive-behavioral group treatment of social phobia. *Behavior Therapy, 33*(1), 5–27. https://doi.org/10.1016/S0005-7894(02)80003-X

Xu, Y., Schneier, F., Heimberg, R. G., Princisvalle, K., Liebowitz, M. R., Wang, S., & Blanco, C. (2012). Gender differences in social anxiety disorder: Results from the national epidemiologic sample on alcohol and related conditions. *Journal of Anxiety Disorders, 26*(1), 12–19. https://doi.org/10.1016/j.janxdis.2011.08.006

Yoshinaga, N., Kobori, O., Iyo, M., & Shimizu, E. (2013). Cognitive behaviour therapy using the Clark & Wells model: A case study of a Japanese social anxiety disorder patient. *Cognitive Behaviour Therapist, 6*, E3. https://doi.org/10.1017/S1754470X13000081

Appendix: Tools and Resources

The following materials for your book can be downloaded free of charge once you register on the Hogrefe website.
Appendix 1: Ryerson Social Anxiety Scales
Appendix 2: Social Anxiety Thought Record
Appendix 3: Exposure and Experiment Monitoring Form

How to proceed:

1. Go to www.hgf.io/media and create a user account. If you already have one, please log in.

2. Go to **My supplementary materials** in your account dashboard and enter the code below. You will automatically be redirected to the download area, where you can access and download the supplementary materials.

    Code: B-6DWYH4

To make sure you have permanent direct access to all the materials, we recommend that you download them and save them on your computer.

Appendix 1: Ryerson Social Anxiety Scales

This is a **preview** of the content that is available in the downloadable material of this book. Please see p. 92 for instructions on how to obtain the full-sized, printable PDF.

Part I: Situations Scale

Please rate your fear or anxiety about being **observed, negatively evaluated, or embarrassed** in the following social situations using the scale below:

0	1	2	3	4
No fear or anxiety	Mild fear or anxiety	Moderate fear or anxiety	Severe fear or anxiety	Extremely severe fear or anxiety

___ 1. Going to parties
___ 2. Speaking in groups
___ 3. Eating or drinking in front of others
___ 4. Giving a formal presentation or speech
___ 5. Going on a date
___ 6. Approaching or speaking with someone you are attracted to
___ 7. Being observed as you walk in late to a class or meeting
___ 8. Being noticed in public spaces, such as on buses or in shopping malls
___ 9. Using public bathrooms with others in the room
___ 10. Being assertive (e.g., saying "no," disagreeing with someone, or objecting to someone's behavior)
___ 11. Working while being observed
___ 12. Being center of attention
___ 13. Making eye contact
___ 14. Making small talk
___ 15. Meeting new people
___ 16. Taking a long time at the front of a line or making others wait (e.g., bank machine, cashier, etc.)
___ 17. Speaking with people in authority
___ 18. Speaking on the telephone
___ 19. People overhearing your conversation
___ 20. Writing in front of people
___ 21. Silences or pauses in conversations
___ 22. Talking about yourself (e.g., personal information or feelings)
___ 23. Showing signs of anxiety in front of other people (*circle all that apply to you*):

    blushing   shaking or trembling   sweating

    looking awkward   losing physical or emotional control   my mind going blank

    forgetting what I'm going to say

___ 24. Other

_____

_____

Only complete Part II if you scored 2 or higher on any item in Part I.

Part II: Severity Scale

For each of the following items, please select the response that best describes your experience.

1. In general, how often do you feel anxious about being observed, negatively evaluated, or embarrassed in social situations?

    0 Never
    1 Rarely
    2 Sometimes
    3 Usually
    4 Always

2. When you felt anxious in the social situations described on the Situations Checklist from Part I, on average, how intense was your anxiety or fear?

    0 No anxiety or fear
    1 Mild
    2 Moderate
    3 Severe
    4 Very severe

3. How much does it bother you that you are anxious in social situations?

    0 Not at all
    1 A little bit
    2 Somewhat
    3 Quite a bit
    4 Extremely

4. How much have you **avoided** engaging in activities of your normal daily life (e.g., getting together with friends, participating in work-related activities, etc.) because you felt anxious about being observed, negatively evaluated, or embarrassed in social situations (before, during, or after the situation)?

    0 Never
    1 Rarely
    2 Sometimes
    3 Usually
    4 Always

5. How frequently do anxiety-provoking social situations come up in your life?

    0 Never
    1 Rarely
    2 Sometimes
    3 Frequently
    4 Very frequently

6. How much does your anxiety in social situations interfere with the following domains of your life? Please use the following scale:

None	Mild	Moderate	Severe	Very Severe
0	1	2	3	3
My anxiety does not interfere with this area of my life at all	My anxiety interferes a little bit with this area of my life	I can still manage in this area of my life, but my anxiety is definitely getting in the way	My anxiety interferes quite a bit with this area of my life and many activities in this domain are impossible for me	My anxiety interferes extremely with this area of my life and most activities in this domain are impossible for me

a) Work/school
b) Friends/social relationships
c) Family life (e.g., parenting, extended family get-togethers)
d) Significant other (e.g., spouse or partner)
e) Home responsibilities (e.g., housework)
f) Leisure activities (e.g., sports, hobbies, volunteering, etc.)
g) Sex life

Part III: History of Social Anxiety

1. At what age did you begin to experience anxiety in social situations? If you have experienced anxiety in social situations for as long as you can remember, please estimate the earliest age at which you recall experiencing anxiety in social situations. _____

2. Do you currently view social anxiety to be a problem for you, in the sense that it interferes with your life or causes you a lot of distress?
   ☐ Yes
   ☐ No

   If yes, at what age did your anxiety in social situations start to become a problem for you, in the sense that it started to interfere with your life or cause you a lot of distress? If you have experienced anxiety in social situations as long as you can remember, please estimate the earliest age at which you recall experiencing distress or interference as a result of your anxiety in social situations. _____

Scoring the RSAS

The **Situations Scale** (part 1) is scored by summing items 1 through 23 (item 24 is not included in the total score. This provides a measure of the breadth of social situations feared by the individual.

The **Severity Scale** is scored by summing items 1 through 6. Item 6 is scored by computing the mean across the 7 life domains (a through g)

The **History of Social Anxiety items** (Part 3) are not included in the scores.

Published Research on the RSAS

Lenton-Brym, A. P., Rogojanski, J., Hood, H. K., Vorstenbosch, V., McCabe, R. E., & Antony, M. M. (2020). Development and validation of the Ryerson Social Anxiety Scales (RSAS). *Anxiety, Stress, and Coping, 33*(6), 642–660. https://doi.org/10.1080/10615806.2020.1771137

Tsekova, V., Lenton-Brym, A. P., Rogojanski, J., Hood, H. K., Vorstenbosch, V., McCabe, R. E., & Antony, M. M. (2021). Psychometric properties of the Ryerson Social Anxiety Scales in individuals with social anxiety disorder. *Anxiety, Stress, and Coping, 34*(5), 559–570. https://doi.org/10.1080/10615806.2020.1870108

Ryerson Social Anxiety Scales © 2019 Jenny Rogojanski, Heather K. Hood, Valerie Vorstenbosch, & Martin M. Antony. Reprinted with permission from the authors.

This is a **preview** of the content that is available in the downloadable material of this book. Please see p. 92 for instructions on how to obtain the full-sized, printable PDF.

Appendix 2: Social Anxiety Thought Record

*This is a **preview** of the content that is available in the downloadable material of this book. Please see p. 92 for instructions on how to obtain the full-sized, printable PDF.*

Day and time	Situation	Anxiety-provoking thoughts and predictions	Anxiety before (0–100)	Alternative thoughts and predictions	Evidence and realistic conclusions	Anxiety after (0–100)

Social Anxiety Thought Record © 2007 Martin M. Antony. Reprinted with permission.

Appendix 3: Exposure and Experiment Monitoring Form

Exposure or experiment *Describe the plan in detail*	Initial anxiety	Anxious predictions *What am I worried will happen?* *How do I think this will go?*	Outcome/learning *What actually happened? Did your feared outcome occur? Did you learn anything useful?*

Peer Commentaries

I highly recommend this clear and comprehensive guide on the nature and treatment of social anxiety disorder. Whether you are a student learning how to assess and treat social anxiety for the first time or a well-seasoned practitioner looking for a refresher on the topic, this helpful book is an essential guide to everything you need to know about evidence-based practice with socially anxious clients. The writing is well organized and easy to digest, and the detailed case illustration brings together all of the important pieces in a highly practical and accessible way. From novices to experts and everyone in between, all practitioners who wish to treat social anxiety in their practice should have a copy of this book on their bookshelf.

David A. Moscovitch, PhD, C Psych, Professor of Clinical Psychology, University of Waterloo, ON, Canada

Focusing on cognitive behavioral approaches, as well as the emotional and relational aspects of the science and art of effectively assessing and treating social anxiety disorder, the authors have produced an accessible evidence-supported compendium of treatment techniques. Clinicians are sure to find the real-world case studies and examples interesting and informative as they begin to apply the treatment.

Peter McEvoy, BSc(hons), MPsych(clin), PhD, Professor of Clinical Psychology, Curtin University and the Centre for Clinical Interventions, Perth, WA, Australia

Once regarded as a neglected psychiatric condition, social anxiety disorder has become a well-researched problem that can be treated effectively with tailored cognitive behavioral therapy strategies. Rowa and Antony are experts in the field who delivered an outstanding book that translates the science into concrete strategies every clinician should be familiar with for their daily work to help people with this disabling and serious problem. I highly recommend this superb book.

Stefan G. Hofmann, PhD, Alexander von Humboldt Professor of Translational Clinical Psychology, Philipps University Marburg, Germany

Advances in Psychotherapy – Evidence-Based Practice

Developed and edited with the support of the Society of Clinical Psychology (APA Division 12)

Series editors
Jonathan S. Comer, PhD
Kenneth E. Freedland, PhD
J. Kim Penberthy, PhD, ABPP
Linda C. Sobell, PhD, ABPP
Danny Wedding, PhD, MPH

- *Practice-oriented*
- *Evidence-based*
- *Expert authors*
- *Easy-to-read*
- *Compact*
- *Cost-effective*

Latest releases

Volume 55

Volume 54

Volume 53

Volume 52

www.hogrefe.com/apt

Advances in Psychotherapy – Evidence-Based Practice

All volumes of the series at a glance

- Affirmative Counseling for Transgender and Gender Diverse Clients (Vol. 45)
- Alcohol Use Disorders (Vol. 10)
- Alzheimer's Disease and Dementia (Vol. 38)
- ADHD in Adults, 2nd ed., (Vol. 35)
- ADHD in Children and Adolescents, 2nd ed. (Vol. 33)
- Autism Spectrum Disorder (Vol. 29)
- Binge Drinking and Alcohol Misuse Among College Students and Young Adults (Vol. 32)
- Bipolar Disorder, 2nd ed. (Vol. 1)
- Body Dysmorphic Disorder (Vol. 44)
- Childhood Depression (Vol. 54)
- Childhood Maltreatment, 2nd ed. (Vol. 4)
- Childhood Obesity (Vol. 39)
- Chronic Illness in Children and Adolescents (Vol. 9)
- Chronic Pain (Vol. 11)
- Depression (Vol. 18)
- Developing Anti-Racist Cultural Competence (Vol. 53)
- Eating Disorders (Vol. 13)
- Elimination Disorders in Children and Adolescents (Vol. 16)
- Family Caregiver Distress (Vol. 50)
- Generalized Anxiety Disorder (Vol. 24)
- Growing Up with Domestic Violence (Vol. 23)
- Harm Reduction Treatment for Substance Use (Vol. 49)
- Headache (Vol. 30)
- Heart Disease (Vol. 2)
- Hoarding Disorder (Vol. 40)
- Hypochondriasis and Health Anxiety (Vol. 19)
- Insomnia (Vol. 42)
- Integrating Digital Tools into Children's Mental Health Care (Vol. 52)
- Internet Addiction (Vol. 41)
- Language Disorders in Children and Adolescents (Vol. 28)
- Mindfulness (Vol. 37)
- Multiple Sclerosis (Vol. 36)
- Nicotine and Tobacco Dependence (Vol. 21)
- Nonsuicidal Self-Injury (Vol. 22)
- Obsessive-Compulsive Disorder in Adults (Vol. 31)
- Occupational Stress (Vol. 51)
- Panic Disorder and Agoraphobia (Vol. 55)
- Persistent Depressive Disorders (Vol. 43)
- Phobic and Anxiety Disorders in Children and Adolescents (Vol. 27)
- Problem and Pathological Gambling (Vol. 8)
- Psychological Approaches to Cancer Care (Vol. 46)
- Public Health Tools for Practicing Psychologists (Vol. 20)
- Sexual Dysfunction in Women (Vol. 25)
- Sexual Dysfunction in Men (Vol. 26)
- Sexual Violence (Vol. 17)
- Social Anxiety Disorder (Vol. 12)
- Substance Use Problems, 2nd ed. (Vol. 15)
- Suicidal Behavior, 2nd ed. (Vol. 14)
- The Schizophrenia Spectrum, 2nd ed. (Vol. 5)
- Time-Out in Child Behavior Management (Vol. 48)
- Treating Victims of Mass Disaster and Terrorism (Vol. 6)
- Women and Drinking: Preventing Alcohol-Exposed Pregnancies (Vol. 34)

Prices: US $29.80 / € 24.95 per volume. Special rates for APA Division 12 and Division 42 members.

www.hogrefe.com/apt